S0-BDP-429

America Hijacked

How Deep State actors from LBJ to Obama killed for money and power, and why they hate Trump so much.

S.M. CARLSON

America Hijacked.

www.AmericaHijackedBook.com

Copyright © 2019 by S. M. Carlson. All rights reserved. Printed in the United States of America. No part of this book may be used or reproduced in any manner whatsoever without written permission except in the case of brief quotations embodied in critical articles and reviews.

For information, contact: S. M. Carlson 1866 E. Market St, C138, Harrisonburg, VA 22801.

This book may be purchased for educational, business, or promotional use.

Cover Art by Ben Garrison - GrrrGraphics.com

For information, please email sales@americahijackedbook.com.

First Edition

978-1-7336755-0-5 (Hardcover)

978-1-7336755-1-2 (Paperback)

Check us out online at www.AmericaHijackedBook.com

Don't forget to review us on Amazon, it really helps!

Thanks

Contents

Forward

America; the greatest country on earth, the land of the free, and home of the brave. This was how I was brought up during the early 80s in sunny Florida. My father was a Deputy Sheriff, and as a younger man, he served honorably in the United States Navy as a Corpsman during Vietnam. I was proud of his sacrifices and service to our country throughout his time in the Navy, and then his continued service to our local community as a police officer. As a child, I hoped to one day follow in his footsteps.

The first Gulf War took place when I was eight years old, and I was still in elementary school at the time. I remember the teachers trying to explain to us in the most simplest of terms what the war represented, and why it was so crucial for our country's freedom. Of course, it was impossible to understand the situation in its context at that age – all I knew, was that there was a bad guy hurting people, and the good guys [the U.S.] were going to stop him. That was all I or my classmates needed to know at the time. We were proud of our men and women in the armed services; we prepared handmade thank you cards and gift baskets for them to show our appreciation.

With the utmost respect for those who have fallen; as a young child, the day-to-day aspects of war were lost on us. I, like my fellow youth of the time, went back to the "more important" things like playing with our Legos, riding our bikes, etc. The adults sheltered us from the negativity and gravity of what war was, giving us just the sugar-coated stories designed to protect us from fear. In retrospect and hindsight, we were too young to understand, and that is fine.

As I continued to grow up and graduate from high school, war was the farthest thing from my mind. We had won the Gulf War when I was a kid, and conflicts like the Battle of Mogadishu never really bubbled up to the top of the current events list for us as children. A child's life in America in the 90s was one full of great prospects for the future and had not a care in the world.

This all came crashing down upon us on that fateful Tuesday morning on September 11th, 2001, when 19 men hijacked four airplanes and crashed two of them into the World Trade Center towers, one into the Pentagon, and a fourth into a field in Pennsylvania. The hijackings served as the first major attack on the U.S. mainland by a foreign enemy since the Post-Civil War era.

We were attacked; life would never be the same for America, and it was up to my generation to take the fight to the animals that attacked us (and kick some serious ass in the process).

It was not very long before I found myself following in my father's footsteps. I enlisted in the U.S. Navy and served during Operations Enduring Freedom and Iraqi Freedom, and I can tell you the U.S. Armed Forces and coalition did their damage.

After returning to civilian life, I started to see a movement led by who I would best describe as "nutjob conspiracy theorists," or as they called themselves, "9/11 Truthseekers," preaching how

9/11 was an inside job. I couldn't believe this; how could these idiots honestly think that the U.S. Government was complicit in the deaths of thousands of American lives? This was utterly unfathomable to me, and for a while, I ignored these whining little brats as they were in obvious need of psychological help.

It would be years later before one of my friends, a self-proclaimed "intellectual freedom fighter" (conspiracy theorist) begged me to watch a few documentaries. I was skeptical to say the least; seriously, how could I believe the illogical dribble from these nutjobs? And yet, he was a friend, so I gave him the respect and at least tried to watch some of the documentaries.

After watching the first documentary; I was not convinced at all. In fact, far from it. I felt that there were clear explanations to all of the "proof" levied in the film, and the producers of the various documentaries that he asked me to watch must have overlooked or misunderstood some of the facts. With this as my mission, I went out to find the answers and disprove these conspiracy theories.

My research opened my eyes to how some very corrupt individuals have taken over our country. Under the power of these individuals, the U.S. has been embroidered in various actions for nearly 100 years that has served to make the elites of the Deep State richer at the expense of the American people.

The complex nature of the human mind is such that people create patterns in facts that do not exist, and this creates some very intricate conspiracy theories. Most of these theories are not rooted in fact, and serve not the goal of finding the truth. Instead, they serve to distort the facts.

In this book, I focus strictly on facts that can be proven, or at a minimum, the ponderance of evidence currently available that would conclude that they are the most likely answer to the question at hand. I will take each issue and systematically analyze them based upon facts, not personal agendas.

It is through this journey of research, interviews, and deliberation that I will take you on throughout this book.

-- Steven

Introduction

Since the first day of recorded history, politicians have taken bribes and profited from their power. We all know that this common practice is *wrong*, but yet we all look the other way. It must be a character flaw in humanity, as we all accept it as something to be expected.

Throughout this book, I will highlight the instances in which our politicians have profited from their power. However, in all honesty, I don't really care if a politician makes a little extra money on the side as long as the end goal is altruistic. I understand this sounds like somewhat of a contradiction, so allow me to explain my reasoning. If there is a contract for the government to purchase *Widgets,* and two competing companies sell the same widget with the same features for the same price, but one company, *Acme Widget Co.* bribes the political elites. In this case, it is entirely understandable in my logic for *Acme Widget Co.* to get the contract. What does it matter if a little "donation" was made to sway the decision making? The only "harm" done was *Some Other Great Widget Co.* did not get the contract. No one was killed, no one was harmed, nothing damaging really took place.

In a perfect world, there would be no corruption, but that is not the world we live in, nor will we ever live in a world without it. If instead of living in a fantasy world, we as a people strive to *primum non nocere* (Latin: "*first, to do no harm*"), then everything else will fall into place. Yes, some will make more money than others, but as long as there is no direct harm to one another, a little profiteering is not the worst thing in the world.

I feel as though the media purposefully dwells on these small instances of corruption, and other similar distractions like which intern the President is "digitally penetrating with a cigar," or which porn-star a President had sex with before running for office. Who really cares? And more importantly, in my opinion; why is the media so focused on these salacious subjects while completing ignoring the real issues at hand, such as corruption that causes wars, assassinations, covering up rapes, financially supporting abhorrent dictatorships, abuse of law enforcement powers against political opponents, and purposeful destruction of the environment; just to increase their wealth and power.

These items are all but ignored by the mainstream media – one must wonder why? Is it possible that the same powerful Deep State elites who are profiting from these abuses of power are the same elites who also own the media? If so, and I believe they are, are they using their media power to purposely distract the masses?

There are a mountain of facts, here. And in fact, too many to give justice to in a single book. For this reason, I have condensed these subjects into a single, concise narrative. I have cited my work and invite you to read in greater detail from those works.

I have strived to keep true to the goal of absolute truth, no matter what the outcome may be. With that in mind, you will find multiple instances in this book where I present the facts and argue both for and against the official account of the events, so that the reader, can make an educated decision on their own. I will also direct you to great books, documentaries, and other resources that provide additional detailed insight into specific subjects.

What this book is not, is an attack on the fine men and women of the U.S. Armed Forces and Law Enforcement communities. I firmly believe they, as a whole, are real heroes that have fought and died serving this country. The truth is that many of these heroes were sent to fight not for the safety of our country, but for the financial profit of few.

The issue at stake here is not a battle of "left" vs " right;" it is simply the Deep State's corruption that has undermined the safety, security, and future of this great country.

Part I:

Background

To understand how the Deep State has usurped power and hijacked our country, we must take a look at the past half-century of American history and international policy.

VIETNAM

The Kennedy Administration had publicly refused to increase tensions and hostilities in regards to the ongoing conflict with North Vietnam. On the heels of JFK's assassination, the incoming President, Lyndon Johnson, was steadfast in his support and desire to reverse the course and push America towards war with North Vietnam. The issue at hand was the politics of going against the late President Kennedy's administration, especially in a time when the American people were very sympathetic towards Kennedy and his legacy.

The solution was to redact and modify current draft security documents prepared by our intelligence agencies for Kennedy and make changes that purported to show the Kennedy administration was aware of the changing situation in Vietnam and that in private, Kennedy was convinced war was inevitable. Many reports and studies were edited to create this false illusion of continuity between the two presidential administrations.

Nowhere is this deception more apparent than in the report of a Honolulu conference on November 20, 1963, and National Security Action Memorandum 273 (NSAM-273). Just two short days after taking the Oath of Office, Johnson met with United States Secretary of Defense, Robert S. McNamara, and other senior leaders to discuss Vietnam. National Security Action Memo 273 was the result of this meeting:

"7. Planning should include different levels of possible increased activity, and in each instance there should be estimates of such factors as:

> *A. Resulting damage to North Vietnam;*
>
> *B. The plausibility of denial;*
>
> *C. Possible North Vietnamese retaliation;*
>
> *D. Other international reaction.*

Plans should be submitted promptly for approval by higher authority. "

The Gulf of Tonkin

The Gulf of Tonkin Incident involved two separate confrontations between the USS Maddox (DD-731) and North Vietnam. Both of these events are collectively referred to in the singular as the Gulf of Tonkin Incident. American reports originally blamed North Vietnam for both incidents, but eventually, more evidence came to light. The situation became very controversial with widespread belief that at least one, and possibly both incidents were either entirely false or their narrative was heavily modified to justify U.S. military action in Vietnam.

The first event took place on the morning of August 2, 1964, with reports that the North Vietnamese Navy sent torpedo boats from their 135th Torpedo Squadron and fired upon the USS Maddox while it was performing a signals intelligence patrol as part of OPLAN 34A[1]. It was reported that the Maddox, in return, initially fired three warning shots before the North Vietnamese boats launched an attack with torpedoes and machine gun fire[2]. During the following fight that ensued, the Maddox expended over 280 3-inch (75 mm) and 5-inch (130 mm) shells; one U.S. aircraft was damaged, and three North Vietnamese boats were damaged. There were no recorded U.S. casualties. However, four North Vietnamese sailors were killed, and six more were wounded.

It was further reported by the U.S. National Security Agency (NSA) that a second Gulf of Tonkin incident occurred two days later on August 4 as another sea battle. However, evidence was quickly found that "Tonkin ghosts" (false radar images) were the cause, and not torpedo boats of the North Vietnamese[3] as had been reported.

Evidence that North Vietnam had attacked the Maddox was still being sought on the night of August 4 when President Johnson addressed the public:

> *"The initial attack on the destroyer Maddox, on August 2, was repeated today by a number of hostile vessels attacking two U.S. destroyers with torpedoes. The destroyers and supporting aircraft acted at once on the orders I gave after the initial act of aggression. We believe at least two of the attacking boats were sunk. There were no U.S. losses."*

Messages recorded that day indicate that both President Johnson and Secretary McNamara had serious concerns towards the validity of the reports[4]. However, they continued with their plans to inform the American people that these attacks on the U.S. posed a grave and immediate danger, and required an immediate military response.

The distorted facts of the Gulf of Tonkin Incident were used as a pretext to escalate the U.S. Armed Forces involvement in the ongoing tensions, with many people calling for all-out war with North Vietnam. On May 4, 1964, William Bundy, Assistant Secretary of State for East Asian and Pacific affairs, called for the U.S. to *drive the communists out of South Vietnam,*" even if that meant attacking both North Vietnam and communist China.

Vietnam People's Army General, Võ Nguyên Giáp, suggested that the Maddox had been sent into the Gulf of Tonkin to provoke an attack from North Vietnam in search of an excuse for escalation and American entry into the war. Various government officials and men aboard the *Maddox* have suggested similar theories[5].

According to Raymond McGovern, a retired CIA officer stated:

> *"[the CIA,] President Lyndon Johnson, Defense Secretary Robert McNamara and National Security Advisor McGeorge Bundy all knew full well that the evidence of any armed attack on the evening of August 4, 1964, the so-called "second" Tonkin Gulf incident, was highly dubious. [...] During the summer of 1964, President Johnson and the Joint Chiefs of Staff were eager to widen the war in Vietnam. They stepped up sabotage and hit-and-run attacks on the coast of North Vietnam."*[6]

This plan was carried out by sending the Maddox, equipped with the latest and most cutting-edge electronic spying technologies, to the Gulf of Tonkin to collect signals intelligence from the North Vietnamese coast. These coastal approaches were seen as a helpful way to get the North Vietnamese to turn on their coastal radars. Once that was accomplished, knowing full well that they were visible on radar, it was authorized to approach the coast as close as 8 miles (13 kilometers) to provoke an attack from North Vietnam.

"The President expects that all senior officers of the government will move energetically to ensure full unity of support for establishing U.S. policy in South Vietnam."[7] Which, in effect, served as a presidential sanctioned extortion, secretly changing Kennedy's plans for withdrawal from Vietnam and ordered all senior officers in the administration to fall in line with the new directive. Simultaneously, this made it appear to the American people that Johnson was following in the footsteps of their beloved Kennedy.

In recorded audio, Johnson said to the former treasury secretary and longtime friend, Robert Anderson:

> *"O.K. Here's what we did: We [were] within their 12-mile [territorial waters] limit, and that's a matter that hasn't been settled. But there have been some covert operations in that area that we have been carrying on-blowing up some bridges and things of that kind, roads and so forth. So I imagine they wanted to put a stop to it. So they come out there and fire and we respond immediately with five-inch guns from the destroyer [Maddox] and with planes overhead. And we cripple them up-knock one of them out and circle the other two. And then we go right back where we were with that destroyer and with another one and plus plenty of planes standing by. And that's where we are now."*[8]

James Bamford, retired United States Navy intelligence analysis writes in his book, *Body of Secrets*, that the primary purpose of the *Maddox*:

> *"was to act as a seagoing provocateur—to poke its sharp gray bow and the American flag as close to the belly of North Vietnam as possible, in effect shoving its five-inch cannons up the nose of the communist navy... The Maddox' mission was made even more provocative by being timed to coincide with commando raids, creating the impression that the Maddox was directing those missions..."*

Thus, the North Vietnamese had every reason to believe that the *Maddox* was involved in these actions.[9]

In 1995, McNamara met with former Vietnam People's Army General, Võ Nguyên Giáp, to find out exactly what happened on August 4, 1964, in the second Gulf of Tonkin Incident. *"Absolutely nothing,"* Giáp replied. Giáp claimed that the attack had been imaginary[10].

In the 2003 documentary, *The Fog of War,* McNamara admitted the August 4 Gulf of Tonkin attack never happened[11].

Through the testimony of some of those involved and the declassification of official government reports, the truth of the fabrications of the Gulf of Tonkin Incident used to justify the war has now come to light. Even though the attacks that happened were not directly provoked, they were a direct result of the OPLAN 34A raids, which was, in essence, an American operation.

It is clear the President knew the attacks in the Gulf of Tonkin were dubious at best, and yet he framed the conversation to the

American people around the idea that we must stand up to the unprovoked aggression of North Vietnam.

I, the author of this book, ponder the intentions of those involved at the time. Were they warmongers only seeking to drum up a new and costly war for their own financial, political, and personal gain? Or were they ideologues that were convinced that the end justifies the means? They knew there were lying about the facts in an effort to improve public support for a war. Would it not have been wiser to address the people, inform them of the [true] facts and explain that war was necessary to remove communist influence in Vietnam? Or were they afraid that their case was not strong enough to convince the public? If their case was not strong, why were they so convinced themselves?

Additional Reading:
- "The Kennedy Assassination and the Vietnam War" by Pete Dale Scott: https://history-matters.com/essays/vietnam/KennedyVietnam1971/KennedyVietnam1971.htm

IRAN-CONTRA AND IRAQ

The Iran-Contra affair involved multiple moving parts in different parts of the world simultaneously.

Mohammad Reza Pahlavi, the last Shah of Iran, was overthrown during the Iranian Revolution on February 11, 1979. The United States was a supporter of the Shah, and was the largest supplier of arms to his country, ultimately helping him maintain power. After his ousting, the Islamic Republic of Iran inherited most of the U.S.-provided weapons and required a constant supply of spare parts from the U.S. to keep them operational. This steady supply stopped when Iranian students stormed the American embassy in Tehran and took 52 Americans hostage in November of 1979. U.S. President Jimmy Carter saw Iran's support for terrorism and imposed an arms embargo on Iran.[12]

The following September, as Iraq invaded Iran, Iran was in desperate need of new weapons and spare parts for their current arsenal to fight off the attack. This put the U.S. in a difficult situation. Both President Carter and incoming President Ronald Reagan went with a policy of blocking arms sales to Iran.

A group of senior Reagan administration officials in the Senior Interdepartmental Group concluded in a secret security briefing report on July 21, 1981 that the arms embargo was mostly ineffective because Iran could always buy arms and spare parts from other countries, such as the Soviet Union. They concluded that the United States should start selling Iran weapons covertly, in order to keep Iran from falling into the Soviet sphere of influence, while also maintaining plausible deniability for the United States.

In the beginning, the U.S. remained neutral after Iraq's invasion of Iran. Although as the war progressed, growing concerns emerged that Iran would get support from the Soviet Union, who was seeking greater regional influence. At the same time, the U.S. also provided resources, political support, and some "non-military" aircraft to Iraq[13] and Iran to prevent either side from striking a clear victory, and fostering a stalemate.

In February of 1982, the U.S. was very concerned that Iran would end up winning the war against Iraq:

> *"[in] a nightmare scenario [...] Iranians invade Iraq, they defeat Iraq, and then head straight for Israel, which is distracted and debilitated by its ongoing adventure in Lebanon," Nick Veliotes, Assistant Secretary of State for Near Eastern and South Asian Affairs[14]*

As a result, the U.S. gradually abandoned its policy of neutrality. The U.S. State Department first removed Iraq from the list of State Sponsors of Terrorism to ease the transfer of dual-use technology.

In March of 1982, Iran began a successful counteroffensive against Iraq (Operation Undeniable Victory), and this forced the U.S. to increase its support for Iraq to prevent Iran from forcing a surrender. President Reagan signed National Security Study Memorandum (NSSM) 4-82 *"review of U.S. policy toward the*

Middle East," and then in June, he signed a National Security Decision Directive (NSDD) co-written by NSC official Howard Teicher, which determined that "*The United States could not afford to allow Iraq to lose the war to Iran.*"[15]

Even though Iraq was originally the instigator, due to the early one-sided support by the U.S., Iran began to win the war over Iraq. This power struggle increased tensions in the region with fears that Iran was becoming too strong, and would end up controlling too large a piece of the middle east. With increased support from the U.S., including billions of dollars' worth of economic aid, military intelligence, dual-use military technology, non-U.S. origin weaponry, and special operations training, the Iraqi military was able to keep Iran in check.[16]

Because of the desire to prevent Iran from taking over Iraq, the CIA turned a blind eye to evidence that Iraq was using chemical weapons against Iran. This is and was a direct violation of International Law[17].

Weapons for Hostages

Even with the Iran-Iraq War ongoing, the U.S. had complex concerns all throughout the region. In early July of 1985 and under a veil of secrecy, Michael Ledeen, a consultant to National Security Adviser Robert McFarlane, requested assistance from Israeli Prime Minister Shimon Peres for help in the sale of arms to Iran.[18] After meeting with an Israeli diplomat by the name of David Kicmche, Leeden and McFarlane confirmed rumors that the Iranians were prepared to have Hezbollah release American hostages in Lebanon in exchange for weapons. [19]

The plan was for Israel to ship weapons through an intermediary (identified as Manucher Ghorbanifar) to the Islamic republic. These weapons would be used to support the supposedly moderate and politically influential Ayatollah Khomeini. At the time, it was believed that he was seeking a rapprochement with the United States. After the transaction, the United States would reimburse Israel with the same weapons, while receiving the monetary benefits from the sale.[20] Under this plan, the U.S. was able to obtain the release of the hostages and profit from the sale of weapons, while also maintaining plausible deniability throughout the entire affair.

In a memo to Shultz and Weinberger, McFarlane wrote:

> *"The short term dimension concerns the seven hostages; the long term dimension involves the establishment of a private dialogue with Iranian officials on the broader relations ... They sought specifically the delivery from Israel of 100 TOW missiles ..."* [21]

Shultz warned Reagan that *"we were just falling into the arms-for-hostages business and we shouldn't do it."*[22]

On August 20, 1985, Israel sent 96 American-made TOW missiles to Iran through an arms dealer, Manucher Ghorbanifar. [23] This was followed up on September 14, 1985, with 408 more TOW missiles. On September 15, 1985, following the second delivery, Reverend Benjamin Weir was released by his captors, the Islamic Jihad Organization.[24] A third delivery, this time on November 24, 1985, 18 Hawk anti-aircraft missiles were delivered.

Almost a year later, on July 26, 1986, Hezbollah freed the American hostage, Father Lawrence Jenco, former head of Catholic Relief Services in Lebanon. Following this, William Casey, head of the CIA, requested that the United States authorize sending a shipment of small missile parts to Iranian military forces as a way of expressing gratitude.[25]

It is interesting to note just how the United States was playing both sides by supporting and Iran and Iraq simultaneously by secretly providing both with weapons. They provided just enough support to guarantee that each side would waste their time and resources, but never win the war.

At the same time, the U.S. government was unofficially supporting Iran. The government's official support for Iraq was not a secret, and was frequently discussed during open sessions of the U.S. Senate and House of Representatives. On June 9, 1992, Ted Koppel reported on ABC's *Nightline* that the *"Reagan/Bush administrations permitted—and frequently encouraged—the flow of money, agricultural credits, dual-use technology, chemicals, and weapons to Iraq."*[26]

Public Disclosure of The Events In Iran

Iranian forces that opposed support from the U.S. became aware of the weapons trade and Mehdi Hashemi, a senior official in the Islamic Revolutionary Guard Corp, leaked the arrangement to the Lebanese magazine *Ash-Shiraa* on November 3, 1986.[27]

The Iranian government confirmed the *Ash-Shiraa* story. Then, ten days later on November 13, President Reagan appeared on television from the Oval Office to address these concerns:

"My purpose was ... to send a signal that the United States was prepared to replace the animosity between [the U.S. and Iran] with a new relationship ... At the same time we undertook this initiative, we made clear that Iran must oppose all forms of international terrorism as a condition of progress in our relationship. The most significant step which Iran could take, we indicated, would be to use its influence in Lebanon to secure the release of all hostages held there."[28]

Nicaragua

While the U.S. was providing weapons and support to both Iraq and Iran, U.S. Marine Corps Lieutenant Colonel and member of the National Security Council, Oliver North, was directing some of those financial gains to Central America in support of the Nicaraguan paramilitary fighters, commonly known as the Contras. At the time, the Contras were waging guerrilla warfare against the democratically-elected, communist-supported, and anti-American, Sandinista government.

Any support by the U.S. of the Contras was a direct violation of the Boland Amendment, where Congress expressly prohibited the U.S. from funding or supporting the Contras:

"None of the funds provided in this Act may be used by the Central Intelligence Agency or the Department of Defense to furnish military equipment, military training or advice, or other support for military activities, to any group or individual ... for the purpose of overthrowing the government of Nicaragua."

The Contras were heavily involved in cocaine trafficking. This was confirmed by multiple intelligence sources on the ground, including one of the Contra leaders in 1985:

> "...told U.S. authorities that his group was being paid $50,000 by Colombian traffickers for help with a 100-kilo cocaine shipment and that the money would go 'for the cause' of fighting the Nicaraguan government."

According to the report, the U.S. State Department paid over $806,000 to *"four companies owned and operated by narcotics traffickers"* to carry humanitarian assistance to the Contras.29

> "I quickly discovered that the Contra pilots were, indeed, smuggling narcotics back into the United States, using the same pilots, planes, and hangers that the Central Intelligence Agency and the National Security Council, under the direction of Lt. Col. Oliver North, used to maintain their covert supply operation to the Contras."30

The full scope of the operation was only known by a few select individuals, that is until the Corporate Air Services HPF821 plane was shot down over Nicaragua on October 5, 1986, by a surface-to-air missile. This U.S. government front-company operated by the CIA contained a cargo of *"60 collapsible AK-47 rifles, 50,000 AK-47 rifle cartridges, several dozen RPG-7 grenade launchers, and 150 pairs of jungle boots."* [31]

Now, part of the mission was in the public eye, and it needed to be covered up before the public knew the full and total truth. In a 'fall on my sword' act, Oliver North destroyed or hid pertinent documents between November 21 and November 25, 1986, that showed the full extent of what was going on in Nicaragua.

During North's trial in 1989, his secretary, Fawn Hall, testified extensively about helping North alter, shred, and remove official United States National Security Council (NSC) documents from the White House. North's explanation for destroying some documents was to protect the lives of the individuals involved in the operations.[32]

After the trial, North was convicted of accepting an illegal gratuity, obstruction of a congressional inquiry, and destruction of documents, but the ruling was overturned because he had been granted immunity.[33]

During his presidential election campaign in 1988, Vice President George H.W. Bush tried to keep his distance from the Iran-Contra affair, and completely denied any knowledge by saying he was *"out of the loop."* Though his diaries included a passage that read as follows:"[he was] *one of the few people that know fully the details."*[34]

Israeli journalist Ronen Bergman claims that Bush not only knew about the weapons sales and drug shipments, but that he was personally briefed by Amiram Nir, a counterterrorism adviser to the Israeli Prime Minister during a visit to Israel:

> *"Nir could have incriminated the incoming President. The fact that Nir was killed in a mysterious chartered airplane crash in Mexico in December 1988 has given rise to numerous conspiracy theories," wrote Bergman.*

Interestingly, on December 24, 1992, and at the end of his term, Bush pardoned the government officials that were found guilty of crimes during the Iran-Contra investigations. It is reasonable to believe that Bush was paying back those that were loyal to him by keeping his involvement a secret.

We will cover more of the Contra side of Iran-Contra both in the Bush Family and Clinton Family chapters. For now, we will focus on the Iran/Iraq side.

IRAQ IN THE 80'S & 90'S

With the Iran-Iraq War officially over, President Bush signed National Security Directives 26, in October of 1989, which said:

> *"Access to Persian Gulf oil and the security of key friendly states in the area are vital to U.S. national security." With respect to Iraq, the directive stated, "Normal relations between the United States and Iraq would serve our longer term interests and promote stability in both the Persian Gulf and the Middle East."[35]*

War With The U.S. Begins

On August 2, 1990, directly against the goals of NSD 26, the Persian Gulf War would officially begin. The U.S., with a coalition of 35 nations, established a defensive position to protect Saudi Arabia from Iraq. President George H. W. Bush said, *"I took this action to assist the Saudi Arabian government in the defense of its homeland,"* asking the American people for their *"support in a decision I've made to stand up for what's right and condemn what's wrong, all in the cause of peace."*

As Scott Peterson reported for *The Christian Science Monitor* in 2002, a key part of the first Bush administration's case, *"was that an Iraqi juggernaut was threatening to roll into Saudi Arabia. Citing top-secret satellite images, Pentagon officials estimated in mid-*

September [of 1990] that up to 250,000 Iraqi troops and 1,500 tanks stood on the border, threatening the key U.S. oil supplier.[36]

Jean Heller of the St. Petersburg Times obtained access to photographs taken by commercial satellites of the same area and time that American intelligence supposedly had found Saddam's Iraqi forces, and was unable to find anything there other than empty desert.

For clarification, she contacted Secretary of Defense, Dick Cheney's office *"for evidence refuting the Times photos or analysis, offering to hold the story if proven wrong."* Their official response, per Heller, was *"Trust us."*[37]

Heller later told Scott Peterson of The Christian Science Monitor that the Iraqi buildup on the border between Kuwait and Saudi Arabia and *"the whole justification for Bush sending troops in there... just didn't exist."*

While the presence of Iraqi military on the Saudi Arabian border was not proven, Iraq did send troops and tanks into Kuwait. This act of aggression into Kuwait by Iraq was condemned universally by the West, but by itself, it did not raise enough public support to send U.S. ground forces into the Middle East.

This was an issue for the Bush Administration's plans. To help with public sentiment; a 15-year old woman by the name of Nayirah, testified to the Congressional Human Rights Caucus in October of 1990. She said that while volunteering at Kuwait's al-Adan hospital, she had seen Iraqi troops remove babies out of their incubators, leaving them *"to die on the cold floor."*[38]

Her first-hand account was so moving, that there was an immediate outcry across the country to send American forces to

Kuwait to rid the country of the Iraqi military[39]. Portions of her testimony were aired that evening on ABC's Nightline and NBC's Nightly News. Representative John Porter commented that never before had he heard such *"brutality and inhumanity and sadism."*[40] Seven U.S. Senators cited her testimony[41] in speeches urging Americans to support the war, and President Bush repeated the story on at least ten separate occasions in the weeks that followed. With the rush of public support, the Bush Administration now had the political capital needed to mobilize ground forces into Kuwait.

The initial conflict to forcibly remove Iraqi troops from Kuwait began with an aerial and naval bombardment on January 17, 1991, and continued for five weeks. The ground assault began on February 24. Without a doubt, this was a clear victory for the coalition forces. Liberating Kuwait and advancing into Iraqi territory with little resistance was a major accomplishment. The coalition ceased its advance and declared a ceasefire 100 hours after the ground campaign started.

The Aftermath of The Gulf War

On March 15, 1991, shortly after Kuwait was liberated, ABC reporter John Martin reported:

> *"patients, including premature babies, did die, when many of Kuwait's nurses and doctors stopped working or fled the country"*[42] *and discovered that Iraqi troops "almost certainly had not stolen hospital incubators and left hundreds of Kuwaiti babies to die."*[43]

In 1992, John MacArthur revealed in *The New York Times* that Nayirah was, in fact, the daughter of Saud Nasir al-Sabah,

Kuwait's ambassador to the U.S., and her testimony had been organized by a group called Citizens for a Free Kuwait, a front for the Kuwaiti government.

Subsequent investigations by Amnesty International, Human Rights Watch/Middle East Watch and independent journalists would show that testimony by Nayirah was entirely bogus[44] and was nothing more than war propaganda designed to increase support for the Persian Gulf War. Andrew Whitley, Director of Middle East Watch, stated:

> *"While it is true that the Iraqis targeted hospitals, there is no truth to the charge, which was central to the war propaganda effort that they stole incubators and callously removed babies allowing them to die on the floor. The stories were manufactured from germs of truth by people outside the country who should have known better."*

Kroll Associates was hired by the Kuwaiti government to investigate the statements of Nayirah and they conducted over 250 interviews throughout a 9-week investigation. The findings were then published in The Kroll Report. In her interviews with Kroll, Nayirah said that she had only personally witnessed a single baby outside its incubator for *"no more than a moment,"* when she had *"stopped by [the hospital] for a few minutes."* In fact, she was never a volunteer there to begin with.[45]

Once again we have found that the U.S. government and top senior officials are guilty of, at a minimum, bending the truth, if not completely falsifying stories as propaganda to convince the American people that war is the only viable option. I, again reaffirm my commentary at the end of the Vietnam chapter of this book. Why wasn't the truth told to Americans by our government? Why were we lied to, just to convince us to go to war? If war was truly necessary, shouldn't the facts clearly outline this truth without the need for fabrication? However, if the truth is not a strong enough burden of evidence, then why are we going to war?

To make things worse, not only was the U.S. government lying to the world during the Iran-Iraq War, but it also supplied Iraq with some very nasty biological weapons.

On February 9, 1994, the Riegle Report by Senator Donald Riegle was released, in which it stated in part:

> *"pathogenic, toxigenic, and other biological research materials were exported to Iraq pursuant to application and licensing by the U.S. Department of Commerce. … These exported biological materials were not attenuated or weakened and were capable of reproduction."*[46]

The report then detailed 70 shipments (including Bacillus anthracis) from the United States to Iraqi government agencies over three years, concluding:

> *"It was later learned that these microorganisms exported by the United States were identical to those the UN inspectors found and recovered from the Iraqi biological warfare program."*[47]

THE SEPTEMBER 11 ATTACKS (9/11)

Early in the morning of Tuesday, September 11, 2001, the World Trade Center in New York, the Pentagon in Washington DC, and a remote field in Pennsylvania were attacked, killing 2,996 people and injuring over 6,000 others.[48] I can still remember that morning vividly; I had recently graduated from High School, and I was at home listening to a local rock station in Tampa, Florida. The morning show crew put aside their normal jokes and took on a very somber tone, informing the listeners that the U.S. was under attack by terrorists in New York. At the time, 24-hour news stations were a pretty new fad, and they were not as popular as they are today. However, they did exist. I flipped on Fox News and was mesmerized by the horror unfolding on the television.

When the first plane crashed, people thought it could have been an accident. And at the time, that seemed completely reasonable. Could it have been just a tragic accident as it was suspected? By the time I became aware of the situation, the second plane had already hit the WTC, and it quickly became obvious that this was a coordinated attack. The news anchors were interviewing various experts on the phone, the term terrorists kept coming up, and at 9:04am, Fox news anchor Jon Scott first mentions the name "Osama bin Laden," and named him as a possible suspect.

"Terrorists? What? Osama bin Laden? Wait, who the hell is that?" Questions like this were running through my head. I was still just an 18-year old kid, and I knew nothing about the world around us.

By 9:15am, NBC had unconfirmed reports from United Airlines that the aircraft was hijacked prior to crashing into the South Tower at the WTC. We knew it was an organized terror attack, and from that point on, America would never be the same.

I still had the radio on in the background, and I could hear the DJ interviewing locals from the Tampa Bay area. Some of the callers stated that they saw Air Force One flying in our area. This was possible, as we were very close to the confirmed location that President Bush was when he was first notified of the attacks. Additional callers stated they had "friends/family/etc." at MacDill AFB, saying that Air Force One was about to land. However, they were redirected at the last minute due to the base being placed on high alert for a possible imminent attack against CENTCOM. The DJ and callers postulated that MacDill would be a logical attack location after the Pentagon was hit. Very quickly, the imaginations of people went wild with only slight glimmers of truth. The situation quickly expanded into wild exacerbations and misinformation.

>**Side bar note**<

Some readers may not be familiar with the Tampa Bay area, and may not know that it is also the home of the United States Central Command (CENTCOM) at MacDill Air Force Base.

I have read conspiracy theories, and while not specifically mentioning the same radio station I was listening to, they have claimed that phone calls such as this were called in by crisis actors to disseminate disinformation. No compelling evidence has been put forward by these theorists, and for this reason, I do not have a lot of confidence in this analysis. It is more reasonable to believe there was not a "vast conspiracy" that could account for the phone calls to the radio station. The risks of having additional persons knowing of the disinformation campaign would outweigh any benefit to any conspirators.

The more likely story is that these callers were normal humans, albeit on the fringe of sanity. However, most were probably completely normal people. They were scared, had bits of second or third-hand information presented to them, and in the absence of the full story, allowed their imaginations to fit fragments of the story and bits and pieces into a storyline that made sense to them. Similar to the telephone game that you probably played as a child, once the story made it to the end of the line, it was a completely different narrative than what was originally spoken to the first person.

I spent the remainder of the day, like most Americans, glued to the TV watching the interviews of various experts as I tried to wrap my brain around what had happened. It would be many years before we had a good glimpse into the truth of that fateful morning. And even today, 17 years later, we have still only scratched the surface of the whole truth.

Based upon the official findings of the 9/11 Commission, we were told that the initial planning phase started in 1996 between Khalid Sheikh Mohammed and Osama Bin Laden[49]. With multiple locations researched, they finalized on the World Trade Center, the Pentagon, and the White House/Capital.[50] There are some conflicting reports on whether the final target was the White House or the U.S. Capitol Building, and because the final plane crashed in the field in Pennsylvania, we may never actually know what the real target was.

Financial Support

The official report by the 9/11 Commission stated:

> *"[the] 9/11 plotters eventually spent somewhere between $400,000 and $500,000 to plan and conduct their attack." They also reported the "origin of the funds remains unknown." and "we have seen no evidence that any foreign government-or foreign government official supplied any funding."*[51]

Privately, however, there were mountains of evidence as to who paid for the attacks. The U.S. government moved very fast to follow the money trail, and within a month of September 11, they identified Yassin al-Qadi, a Saudi Arabian businessman with extensive financial ties to Chicago as one of Osama bin Laden's primary financiers.[52]

In an interview with *Computerworld Magazine*, a former business associate described his relationship with Yassin al-Qadi as follows:

"I met him a few times and talked to him a few times on the telephone. He never talked to me about violence. Instead, he talked very highly of his relationship with [former President] Jimmy Carter and [Vice President] Dick Cheney."[53]

The Muwafaq Foundation, which American authorities have confirmed was an arm of bin Laden's terror organization, was headed by Yassin al-Qadi,[54] who was also known as the owner of Ptech – a company that has supplied high-tech computer systems to the FBI, the Internal Revenue Service, the United States Congress, the United States Army, the Navy, the Air Force, the North Atlantic Treaty Organization, the Federal Aviation Administration (FAA), and the White House. Multiple other individuals with suspected radical ideologies including Yacub Mirza and Hussein Ibrahim. The latter of whom served as the Vice President and Chief Scientist of Ptech and was also the Vice Chairman of a now-defunct investment group called BMI, which the FBI has named as a conduit used by al-Qadi to launder money to Hamas militants.[55]

Former FBI agent Robert Wright Jr. told ABC's, Brian Ross:

"September 11th is a direct result of the incompetence of the FBI's International Terrorism Unit," specifically referring to the Bureau's hindering of his investigation into Yasin al-Qadi.[56]

According to Senator Bob Graham, Chairman of the Senate Intelligence Committee:

"Two of the Sept. 11, 2001, hijackers had a support network in the United States that included agents of

the Saudi government, and the Bush administration and FBI blocked a congressional investigation into that relationship ... a direct line between the terrorists and the government of Saudi Arabia, and an attempted coverup by the Bush administration."[57]

In Graham's book, Intelligence Matters, he makes clear that some details of that financial support from Saudi Arabia were part of a block of 27 pages in the 9/11 Commission's final report that were blocked from public release by the administration, despite the pleas of both parties on the House and Senate intelligence committees.[58]

Mujahideen and The Soviet-Afghan War

Before we go much further into the 9/11 attacks, we should cover the Mujahideen, the Soviet-Afghan War, and the rise of Osama Bin Laden.

The Soviet-Afghan War lasted just over nine years, from December 1979 until February 1989. It was fought in the mountainous regions of Afghanistan with the main goal of driving the Soviet Army out of the region. The Afghans were supported by the United States, Saudi Arabia, and Pakistan with weaponry and financial support, essentially turning these battles into a proxy war of the Cold War. Without this support, the Soviets would have easily won the war against Afghanistan.

The local Arab men fought a guerrilla-style war and called themselves Mujahideen, the plural form of mujahid, the term used for one engaged in Jihad ("holy war"). One of the young Arab men fighting in the Mujahideen was a young Saudi named Osama bin Laden. He was the son of a wealthy Saudi family that owned multiple successful businesses in the construction and oil industries. While not a supporter of the Western World, he was indifferent to them. It was not until the buildup to the first Iraq War (The Persian Gulf War/Iraq War I) when he and his fighters went to the Saudis and told them that the Arabs should protect their lands, not the godless infidels of the west as he thought of the U.S. and their allies. When the Saudis in turn asked for assistance from the U.S., bin Laden took this as an insult and he vowed revenge. Under his leadership, bin Laden formed al-Qaeda.

Prior Intelligence of 9/11 Attacks

In late 1999, the NSA intercepted a telephone call mentioning a meeting between al-Qaeda associate Walid bin Attash ("Khallad") and Khalid al-Mihdhar. They discussed setting up an in-person meeting in Kuala Lumpur, Malaysia with Nawaf al-Hazmi and Abu Bara al Yemeni. At the time of this meeting, the agency determined:

> "*something nefarious might be afoot,* "and yet, it still took no further action.[59]

The CIA had already been alerted by Saudi intelligence to the status of Mihdhar and Hazmi as al-Qaeda members, and a CIA team had broken into Mihdhar's Dubai hotel room and discovered that Mihdhar had a U.S. visa.

Two of these men, al-Mihdhar, and al-Hazmi would end up being two of the five hijackers of American Airlines Flight 77, the plane that was deliberately flown into the Pentagon. Al Yemeni was planned to be part of the attacks, however, he was unable to obtain a U.S. Visa and could not participate directly.

Malaysian intelligence observed the meeting between these men and informed the CIA that they were flying to Bangkok, but the CIA never notified other agencies. An FBI liaison to Alec Station asked permission to inform the FBI of the meeting, but was told that "*This is not a matter for the FBI.*"[60]

By late June, senior counter-terrorism official, Richard Clarke, and CIA Director George Tenet were *convinced that a major series of attacks was about to come.* Although, the CIA believed that the attacks would likely occur in Saudi Arabia or Israel.[61] Clarke would later write that:

> *"Somewhere in CIA there was information that two known al-Qaeda terrorists had come into the United States... in [the] FBI there was information that strange things had been going on at flight schools in the United States... They had specific information about individual terrorists... None of that information got to me or the White House."*[62]

In late 1999, SOCOM (Special Operations Command) began a highly classified data-mining operation named Able Danger, and by January of 2000, the team had identified an al-Qaeda terrorist cell in Brooklyn and identified a man by the name of Atta as a member.[63] On at least three separate occasions in mid-2000, Captain Phillpot asked his superiors for permission to bring the FBI into the investigation. Each request was denied by military lawyers due to claims that the data they were harvesting may not be legal to disclose. This left the FBI unaware of the cell in Brooklyn.[64]

Thomas Kean and Lee Hamilton, co-chairs of the 9/11 Commission, both stated that Able Danger was not *"historically significant."*[65]

One day before a 2005 US Senate hearing, key members of the Able Danger team were hit with a gag order by Secretary of Defense Donald Rumsfeld,[66] preventing them from telling the Senators the truth that Able Danger had detected a terrorist cell and Mr. Atta.[67] One member of the team that was able to provide limited testimony was Erik Kleinsmith, Army Major and the Chief of Intelligence of the Land Information Warfare Activity. He testified in May or June of 2000, a year before the 9/11 attacks, and was ordered to destroy over 2.5 terabytes of Able Danger data.[68]

Why was this information deleted just prior to 9/11? Was it because they stumbled across details of the upcoming attack and high ranking officials did not want those details to be known? Or was it just pure happenstance? I cannot imagine a valid reason that the SOCOM would want information that could point to a possible attack disposed of, even if they had little confidence in the results.

In June 2001, a *"high-placed member of a U.S. intelligence agency"* told BBC reporter Greg Palast that *"after the [2000] elections, the agencies were told to 'back off'* investigating the bin Laden family and Saudi royals."[69]

In July, a Phoenix-based FBI agent, Kenneth Williams, sent a message to FBI headquarters and to FBI agents in New York, alerting them to *"the possibility of a coordinated effort by Osama bin*

Laden to send students to the United States to attend civil aviation universities and colleges." [70]

On July 10, Richard Blee, head of CIA's al Qaeda unit, requested an emergency meeting with National Security Advisor Condoleezza Rice, and informed her:

"There will be significant terrorist attacks against the United States in the coming weeks or months. The attacks will be spectacular. They may be multiple." [71]

Blee recommended to Rice:

"Getting into the Afghan sanctuary, launching a paramilitary operation, creating a bridge with Uzbekistan." [72]

On August 6th, the CIA's Presidential Daily Brief designated "For the President Only," was entitled *"Bin Ladin [Laden] Determined to Strike in U.S."* The memo noted that *"The FBI information ... indicates patterns of suspicious activity in this country consistent with preparations for hijackings or other types of attacks."* [73]

In mid-August, one Minnesota flight school alerted the FBI to Zacarias Moussaoui, who had asked "suspicious questions." The FBI found that he was a radical who had traveled to Pakistan, and the INS arrested him for overstaying his French visa. Their request to search his laptop was denied by FBI headquarters due to the lack of probable cause. [74] The FBI did arrest Moussaoui on an immigration violation, but not until after the 9/11 attacks. On December 11, 2001, Moussaoui was indicted by a federal grand jury on six felony charges: conspiracy to commit acts of terrorism transcending national boundaries, conspiracy to commit aircraft piracy, conspiracy to destroy aircraft, conspiracy to use weapons of mass destruction, conspiracy to murder United States employees, and conspiracy to destroy property.

It is clear that various American and international intelligence agencies knew that Osama bin Laden was planning an attack, most likely in the U.S. It was also known that his supporters had the intention of using planes as weapons against building(s), and that members of their terrorist organization were enrolled in flight schools in the U.S.. The issue appeared to be in artificial walls between various intelligence and law enforcement agencies that prevented the information from coming together into a single narrative.

I do not feel that there was a vast conspiracy that permeated across the entire U.S. government that allowed these attacks to be successful. However, I do feel that it's important to ask the question, "did some purposefully turn a blind eye to some key pieces of information to better strengthen their personal goals?" Yes, it is clear from the evidence that this is the truth. Notwithstanding, the single greatest reason the 9/11 attacks took place and were successful, is how the various government agencies were more concerned about turf wars between agencies and the personal careers of themselves, rather than working together to prevent a possible attack.

WTC Tower Collapse

I will not spend a lot of time covering the collapse of the twin towers in this book. You might be wondering why? The answer to this question is both simple, and complex at the same time – allow me to explain.

The *9/11 Commission Report,* released in 2004, made some incomprehensibly ignorant claims about the tower collapse. More specifically, they made a claim that the towers suffered from a self-invented term of "pancake collapse," where they state that the *"interior core of the buildings was a hollow steel shaft, in which elevators and stairwells were grouped."*[75] This completely ignores the fact there were 47 massive structural steel supports in each tower. If the pancake collapse had taken place, you would have observed the floors pancaking on top of themselves *around* the core, leaving the massive steel core intact after the floors fell away from them.

The official investigation by the National Institute of Standards and Technology (NIST) concluded that the buildings collapsed as a result of the impacts of the planes, and the fires that resulted.[76] I have a strong disagreement with the narrative and explanation by NIST. However, I do concede that I am not a structural engineer and cannot speak intelligently on this subject. NIST states, in part, that the construction of the twin towers was quite unique, in that it deviated from standard construction practices at the time by bringing the structural supports normally found throughout a specific floor, and relocating them to the center and outside walls.

FDNY Chaplain Father John Delendick, said that after the top of the South Tower appeared to explode, he asked FDNY Chief Ray Downey if jet fuel had blown up. Downey "a *very respected expert on building collapse,"*[77] replied "*[he] thought there were bombs up there because it was too even,"*[78] referring to how symmetrical the explosions were and logically cannot be produced by exploding jet fuel[79].

Architects & Engineers for 9/11 Truth, a non-profit organization founded by Richard Gage, a San Francisco Bay area architect, along with a coalition of structural engineers and architects argue that the buildings of the World Trade Center could not have collapsed as a result of only the impact made from the planes,[80]or as a result of the fires that had been caused by them. Rather, they claim to have identified additional evidence pointing to an explosive demolition of the World Trade Center buildings.[81]

Gage criticized NIST for not having investigated the complete sequence of the collapse of the World Trade Center towers[82] and claims that, *"the official explanation of the total destruction of the World Trade Center skyscrapers has explicitly failed to address the massive evidence for explosive demolition."*[83]

He further argues that the buildings of the World Trade Center could not have collapsed at the speed that has been observed without first tearing apart several columns of their structures with the help of explosives.[84]

He maintains that the *"sudden and spontaneous"* collapse of the towers would have been impossible without a controlled demolition, and that pools of molten iron found in the debris of the buildings were evidence of the existence of the explosive thermite.[85]

While conceding that I do not have the educational background in structural engineering nor controlled demolition, their explanations appear to me, a layman, to be the most plausible. I invite the readers to review their evidence on their website at www.ae911truth.org.

Additional experts conclude similar findings, including physicist Steven Jones: *"evidence points overwhelmingly to the conclusion that all three buildings were destroyed by controlled demolition."*[86]

WTC Building 7 Collapse
_____

With all due respect to those that died in the towers, a subject that I find more interesting than the collapse of the twin towers, is the fact that WTC Building 7 collapsed. A building that was not hit by planes and sustained far less damage than other surrounding buildings in the WTC complex when the twin towers fell also collapsed. Remember, those other buildings all stood. NIST's explanation stated that the collapse of Building 7 was due to fires that burned uncontrolled throughout the day. They also stated that diesel fuel stored at the building did not play an important role, nor did the structural damage from the collapse of the twin towers.[87]

Building 7 was the first, excluding for the moment the twin towers, steel construction building to ever fall primarily as a result of uncontrolled fires.[88] In comparison to the twin towers, Building 7 was a standard steel frame constructed building without any unique structural design aspects that could possibly account for the collapse of this building. Even if in the most unlikely of possible scenarios the twin towers fell due to their design, there is zero reason a similar catastrophic failure could have caused the collapse of Building 7.

To support its position, Architects & Engineers for 9/11 Truth points to the *"free fall"* acceleration of Building 7 during part of the collapse[89] to *"lateral ejection of steel,"* and to *"mid-air pulverization of concrete."*[90]

> *"Among the most egregious examples is the explanation for the collapse of WTC 7 as an elaborate sequence of unlikely events culminating the almost symmetrical total collapse of a steel frame building into its own footprint at free-fall acceleration."*[91]

Lies in The NIST Report

NIST claims that no one, including bystanders, media, NYPD, nor NYFD reported hearing or seeing explosions before, during, or after the attacks on the towers.[92] This is a blatant lie, as well over 100 NYFD firefighters reported hearing sounds of explosions,[93] as did countless members of the media, NYPD, and WTC employees[94].

NIST claims that the towers fell as a direct result from the damage sustained by the impact of the jet aircraft and the subsequent fires that burned, and that no explosives were needed, nor used.[95] The problem with this assessment by NIST, is that the towers were specifically engineered to handle impacts from aircraft of similar size,[96] due to the proximity to nearby Newark Liberty International Airport and LaGuardia Airport. This also ignores the fact that jet fuel, nor office fires that only reached 1,800 degrees Fahrenheit at the maximum, can generate enough heat to melt steel, which requires temperatures greater than 2,700 degrees Fahrenheit[97].

NIST originally claimed that WTC 7 collapsed due to a raging inferno fed by massive storage tanks filled with diesel fuel.[98] However, after some deeper investigation, even NIST realized the absurdity of this claim, and removed the claim for diesel fuel, stating nothing more than *"the first known instance of the total collapse of a tall building primarily due to fires."*[99] This is about as close to a direct admission that their claims are completely fabricated that we may ever see, explicitly claiming that they cannot find any other steel frame structure in history to ever fail in this manner.

In Summary

After all of my research, it is clear that there is more to the WTC attack and collapse than the official story is able to explain. Furthermore, it is highly likely that explosives were used within the twin towers and in Building 7. The questions to ask now are, "how did the explosives get into the building and why were they placed there?" and "who benefited from all three buildings collapsing?"

We were told that Osama bin Laden and Al-Qaeda are to blame for the attacks[100], yet the FBI did not list 9/11 as one of the crimes for which he was wanted.[101] When pressed, the FBI stated that they had "no hard evidence" to link bin Laden to the attacks.[102]

Putting the FBI aside for the moment, if we accept it as fact that he was responsible for planning the attack, then how did they get explosives into the buildings? If they planned on using explosives for the destruction of the buildings, why waste time with the planes? Why not just rig the explosives and blow up the buildings? Why all the theatrics with crashing planes? Did they want the collapses to take place on live TV to have a larger emotional impact? These later questions, while interesting to postulate, are of less importance than the first question. Everything comes down to this: "How did they get these explosives into the buildings?"

There are few conspiracy theories that state that President Bush's brother, Marvin Bush, was the owner/principle for the company Securacom that provided security for WTC, United Airlines, and Dulles International Airport. While an interesting theory, I was unable to find any concrete evidence of these claims, short of conspiracy theory websites quoting each other.

Interesting to note, all three buildings were leased by the same person, Larry Silverstein, and he had just leased the three buildings a few short weeks prior. After a lengthy court battle with his insurance company, he was paid $7 billion in damages for the buildings, a staggering return on his initial investment of a mere $15 million. The collapse of the buildings also saved him an estimated $1 billion in environmental cleanup costs to remove asbestos from the buildings and replace with more modern materials.

Additional theories that are verified in testimonials by persons in the building stated that there were a number of "power downs" and security/fire upgrades to the same floors hit by the planes just a few short weeks earlier[103].

Daria Coard, 37, a guard at the North Tower, said an enhanced security detail that included bomb-sniffing dogs had been working 12-hour shifts for the past two weeks because of numerous phone threats. But on Thursday, September 6, 2001, the bomb-sniffing dogs were abruptly removed.

Once again, if we are able to take these theories at their face value, it seems quite suspicious, and it would also provide a viable avenue for installing explosives into the buildings. Unfortunately, we may be unable to verify exactly how and by whom the explosives were placed. All we know for sure is that they were placed there and detonated by someone.

I postulate that it is possible senior members of U.S. intelligence agencies, up to and including the Bush administration, wanted this attack to take place for one reason for another, and they either turned a blind eye to the evidence or actively participated to guarantee a successful outcome to this terrorist operation. What individual or what country would benefit most from a war in the Middle East? Or, perhaps it is possible that a third-party country, such as Saudi Arabia or Israel, also wanted the U.S. to enter into a prolonged Middle Eastern war, so they covertly rigged the buildings with explosives and allowed the al-Qaeda plot to take place in hopes of using bin Laden as a scapegoat for the blame?

We know from the *Prior Intelligence* section above, that individuals privy to the full 9/11 Commission report claim that there was ample evidence to blame Saudi Arabia for their financial support. However, for the sake of international diplomacy, it was classified and not presented in the public release of the report.

In an effort of brevity to keep this manuscript concise and to the point of my overarching thesis of the corruption that has hijacked America, I will keep the analysis of the WTC attacks short. I invite you to read the documents on www.ae911truth.org to get more details.

- An excellent timeline of events can be found at: https://en.wikipedia.org/wiki/Timeline_for_the_day_of_the_September_11_attacks
- Architects & Engineers for 9/11 Truth: www.ae911truth.org
- Video Summary of Building 7 collapse: https://www.ae911truth.org/evidence/videos/video/2-architects-and-engineers-solving-the-mystery-of-building-7
- Pilots for 9/11 Truth: www.pilotsfor911truth.org

OPERATIONS ENDURING FREEDOM AND IRAQI FREEDOM

After the Soviets withdrew from Afghanistan, the area plunged into numerous battles for power. While still in power, Northern Alliance leader, Abdur Rab Rasool Sayyaf, invited Osama bin Laden to live in his country, thinking he would be able to assist in preventing the Taliban from taking over the country.[104] Instead, bin Laden forged an alliance between the Taliban and his al-Qaeda organization. Together, their extreme interpretation of Islamic law prompted them to ban music, television, sports, drugs, and dancing, and enforce harsh judicial penalties.

Responding to the 9/11 attacks, President George W. Bush announced on October 7, 2001, that he would be taking the fight to al-Qaeda and the Taliban, and began with airstrikes in Afghanistan[105].

Opium

In the 1980s, Afghanistan was producing less than 1% of the world's supply of opium. Once the CIA began to assist the Mujahideen in the fight against the Soviets, the industry quickly grew to 40% of the world's supply. By 1999, over 3,200 tons of heroin a year, accounting for around 80% of the market, was produced and shipped worldwide[106]. A fact that is not very well published by mainstream media is that once in power, the Taliban cut the production of heroin down to less than 185 tons annually.

Once the coalition forces pushed the Taliban out of Afghanistan, production of heroin quickly shot up, and by 2007, more than 92% of the world's heroin supply[107] came from the region.

Taking The Battle To Iraq

When President Bush attacked Afghanistan, he had the strong support and backing of the American people behind him to go after and bring to justice the individuals responsible for the 9/11 attacks. This support was stretched very thin when they transitioned from Afghanistan to Iraq. Many Americans wondered why the U.S. was now attacking Iraq.

For the Bush administration, redirecting public attention to Iraq had the added benefit of distracting critics from focusing on the embarrassing facts of the 9/11 attacks that were coming to light. Whistleblowers were coming forward and investigative journalists were digging into the facts, and it was quickly becoming known that 9/11 was far more complicated than nineteen men hijacking planes and crashing them into buildings. Fifteen of the nineteen reported hijackers were Saudi nationals. What could or should the Saudi government have known about or done to prevent these attacks? What about the deep relations between the Saudi royal family and the Bush family? Or how the Bush administration quickly flew members of the Saudi royal family and the bin Laden family out of the U.S. hours after the 9/11 attacks, overruling the FAA order to ground all non-military and non-emergency responder flights? These are all issues that W.

removed from the public sphere, and a war in Iraq was the perfect distraction.

In the months leading up to the invasion of Iraq, President Bush and members of his administration indicated that they possessed information demonstrating a link between Saddam Hussein and al-Qaeda. Stating:

> *"Iraq could decide on any given day to provide a biological or chemical weapon to a terrorist group or individual terrorists. Alliance with terrorists could allow the Iraqi regime to attack America without leaving any fingerprints."[108]*

Newsweek magazine published a story about Saddam Hussein and al-Qaeda joining forces to attack U.S. interests in the Gulf Region. ABC News broadcast a story of this link soon after.[109]

Vice President Dick Cheney told *Meet the Press* on December 9, 2001, that Iraq was harboring Abdul Rahman Yasin, a suspect in the 1993 World Trade Center bombing,[110] and repeated the statement in another appearance on September 14, 2003, saying:

> *"We learned more and more that there was a relationship between Iraq and al-Qaida that stretched back through most of the decade of the '90s, that it involved training, for example, on BW and CW, that al-Qaida sent personnel to Baghdad to get trained on the systems that are involved. The Iraqis providing bomb-making expertise and advice to the al-Qaeda organization. We know, for example, in connection with the original World Trade Center bombing in '93 that one of the bombers was Iraqi, returned to Iraq*

after the attack of '93. And we've learned subsequent to that, since we went into Baghdad and got into the intelligence files, that this individual probably also received financing from the Iraqi government as well as safe haven."[111]

In an interview with National Public Radio in January 2004, Cheney stated that there had been "*overwhelming evidence*" of a relationship between Saddam and al-Qaeda based on evidence including Iraq's purported harboring of Yasin.[112]

Notwithstanding the official stance of the Bush administration, the consensus of intelligence experts has been that Saddam Hussein and al-Qaeda never established an operational relationship, and that consensus is backed up by reports from the independent 9/11 Commission and by declassified Defense Department reports.[113] In addition, the Senate Select Committee on Intelligence published in 2006, phase II of its investigation into prewar intelligence reports. They concluded that there was no evidence of ties between Saddam Hussein and al-Qaeda.[114]

On April 29, 2007, former Director of Central Intelligence George Tenet, said on *60 Minutes*, "*We could never verify that there was any Iraqi authority, direction, and control, complicity with al-Qaeda for 9/11 or any operational act against America, period.*"[115]

Year after the invasion of Iraq, a leaked memo speaking of Iraq and the possibility of weapons of mass destruction (WMDs) clearly outlined the falsehood of the narrative when it stated: "*the intelligence and facts are being fixed around the policy.*"[116] The policy, of course, was the desire to remove Saddam Hussein from power. The London's Sunday Times immediately wrote about this memo once word was out, but US-based media buried the story for weeks and only reluctantly wrote about it in a dismissive way, never mentioning the key phrase that intelligence was "fixed."

Part II:

The Conspirators

In Part I, we went over just a few of the questionable actions that the powerful elites have taken throughout the last seventy plus years. Now, we will go over some of the individuals responsible for these actions and how these wars have increased their power and wealth.

THE BUSH FAMILY DYNASTY

The Bush family is an American dynasty in every meaning of the word. Peter Schweizer, the author of a biography on the family, has described the Bushes as *"the most successful political dynasty in American history."*[117] They are involved in politics, sports, entertainment, oil, and many other industries, with an untold vast net worth that started back with former President George H. W. Bush's father, Prescott Bush, who profited over $1.5 million dollars from forced labor camps in Auschwitz[118].

> *"George Bush's grandfather, the late US Senator Prescott Bush, was a director and shareholder of companies that profited from their involvement with the financial backers of Nazi Germany.*
>
> *The Guardian has obtained confirmation from newly discovered files in the US National Archives that a firm of which Prescott Bush served as a director was involved with the financial architects of Nazism.*
>
> *His business dealings, which continued until his company's assets were seized in 1942 under the Trading with the Enemy Act, has, more than 60 years later, led to a civil action for damages in Germany against the Bush family by two former slave labourers at Auschwitz, and to a hum of pre-election controversy.*

The evidence has also prompted one former US Nazi war crimes prosecutor to argue that the late Senator's action should have been grounds for prosecution for giving aid and comfort to the enemy."[119]

[Vesting Order Number 248]

**ALL OF THE CAPITAL STOCK OF UNION BANK-
ING CORPORATION AND CERTAIN INDEBTED-
NESS OWING BY IT**

Under the authority of the Trading with the enemy Act, as amended, and Executive Order No. 9095, as amended,[1] and pursuant to law, the undersigned, after investigation, finding:

(a) That the property described as follows:

All of the capital stock of Union Banking Corporation, a New York corporation, New York, New York, which is a business enterprise within the United States, consisting of 4,000 shares of $100 par value common capital stock, the names of the registered owners of which, and the number of shares owned by them respectively, are as follows:

Names	Number of shares
E. Roland Harriman	3,991
Cornelius Lievense	4
Harold D. Pennington	1
Ray Morris	1
Prescott S. Bush	1
H. J. Kouwenhoven	1
Johann G. Groeninger	1
Total	4,000

[1] 7 F.R. 5205.

Director of the CIA (George H. W. Bush)

As the Director of the CIA, George H. W. Bush was a highly skilled and accomplished liar that performed his craft with the utmost skill of an artistic expression:

"...he had perfected the bending and stretching of truth... George was as smooth as an eel slithers through

oil. His lies on behalf of the CIA ranged from outright falsehoods and adamant denials to obfuscations and evasive omissions."[120]

But what else should you expect from a former CIA Director? He is, after all, a professional liar and spy. That, in and of itself, does not make a person good, nor bad; it is simply who they are. It does, however, bring into question the authenticity and honesty of many statements made by H. W. throughout his professional and political career.

After President Carter forced H. W. to step down as the CIA Director, he spent the next few years building a team of current and EX-CIA operatives to work together to not only destroy Carter's chances of reelection, but to also place him in the White House. Key to his strategy, was preventing Carter from obtaining the political win if the American hostages held in Iran were released during Carter's administration.[121] If Bush were to successfully convince Iran to hold off until after election day, this hot-topic issue would single-handedly kill Carter's chances of reelection, and that is exactly what happened. After promising billions of dollars of U. S. military assets to Iran and $40 million in cash bribes to Iranian officials,[122] Carter lost the election. Then, on January 20, 1981, the very same day that Reagan/Bush was sworn into office, the hostages were released by Iran[123].

Years later in 1992, the National Review released an investigative report that stated: *"through FBI and CIA documents released ... Bush played a personal role in keeping the hostages in Khomeini's hands until after Election Day 1980."*

Going back for a moment to the Iran-Contra scandal we covered back in Part I, the reader may remember that Bush was VP during this time, and claimed that he had no knowledge of the operations going on in Nicaragua. Yet, in December 1983, Bush and Oliver North both flew down to El Salvador to meet with local army officers to encourage them to attack Nicaragua covertly on behalf of the U.S. Why would he fly there to seek the support for a battle he had no knowledge of? Additionally, the CIA launched numerous raids on Nicaragua under Bush's orders between January and March of 1984.[124]

Further evidence that Bush was not only fully aware of, but was actually heading the direct supervision of the Contra situation was after one of the planes run by a CIA front company was shot down over El Salvador with 10,000 lbs. of small arms, ammunition, and hand grenades as its payload. The pilot Eugene Hasenfus, called VP Bush to inform him that the mission had failed.[125] This flight's mission was the same as previous flights; to bring weapons to the Contras and return to the U.S. with cocaine and marijuana to a small airport in Mena, Arkansas.[126] Another Deep State actor, Bill Clinton, was serving as the Governor of Arkansas, and he provided "approval and protection" for the flights coming and going 24/7.[127]

If the plane was never shot down, we may have never found out about the illicit scheme.

Once news of the downed cargo plane in El Salvador hit the wire, the political ramifications were quickly coming to light. Immediately, the disinformation and spin campaign kicked into overdrive to protect the VP and divert knowledge of the CIA's ownership of the C-123k cargo plane. Oliver North's own diary clearly mentioned the VP and his involvement: "*Felix [Rodriguez] is talking too much about the Vice President's connection.*"[128]

This wouldn't be the only time that VP Bush's name came up in regards to drug smuggling from Nicaragua to Arkansas. One of the pilots by the name of Barry Seal was caught by the IRS and charged with tax evasion for his profits made by smuggling cocaine into the U.S.. During the investigation, Seal was covertly recorded saying:

> "*Ever hear of that expression 'it's not what you know, it's who you know?' Well, whoever said that just hadn't caught the Vice President's kids in the dope business, 'cause I can tell you for sure what you know can definitely be more important than who you know. [...] Fuck, I even got surveillance video catchin' the Bush boys red-handed. I consider this stuff my insurance policy.*"

This conversation referred to Jeb Bush picking up multiple kilos of cocaine.[129] It was not long after this recording that Barry was found dead by multiple gunshot wounds. The FBI quickly confiscated a box in Barry's vehicle, which was suspected to contain the video evidence against Jeb. It was reported by Barry's secretary that he was known to keep important papers and blackmail in his trunk. She further claimed, "*Barry Seal died with Vice President Bush's phone number in the trunk of his car.*"[130]

Ross Perot obtained evidence of CIA-backed cocaine smuggling and attempted to get VP Bush's attention, but he was ignored. He would later claim "[all I] *got from Bush was a grim smile.*"[131]

The VP Wants To Be President

While in the White House as VP, Bush set his sights on the Presidency. He and many of his closest supporters felt that winning a general election would be very challenging and possibly unobtainable. With this in mind, it is rumored that Bush worked behind the scenes to have Reagan assassinated. This claim is not taken lightly by the author, and I found some evidence that pointed to the affirmative and some that are very dubious at best as to whether or not Bush had conspired or not.

An undisputed fact is that the Bush family and the family of would-be assassin John Hinckley had close connections,[132] including a pre-scheduled dinner between VP Bush's son Neil and John's brother Scott Hinckley to take place the day after the assassination attempt. Neil Bush told the Houston Post that "*he knew the Hinckley family because they had made large contributions to the Vice President's campaign.*" [133]

Political author Roger Stone, interviewed by Rich Zeoli on Talk Radio 1210 WPHT during his research for his book *Jeb! And the Bush Crime Family* uncovered evidence that claims:

> "*There are two shooters in the Reagan assassination attempt, not one. I give you photographic evidence and eyewitness evidence of a second man standing on a balcony holding a gun, who can clearly be seen in the uncropped photos and I traced many of the*

connections of the Bushes to the Hinckleys. It's more than you've been told.

[...]

I think it is more than possible because one has to understand the backdrop here and that is this story is missing from Bill O'Reilly's Killing Reagan book entirely. Al Haig, Reagan's Secretary of State and Vice President George Bush are fighting over control of foreign policy. George 'Poppy' Bush is for the 'New World Order.' Haig has the quaint notion that he's Reagan's man. This is supposed to be Reagan's foreign policy, more conservative than what Bush wants. There are two different executive orders sitting on Reagan's desk. One giving authority to Haig. One giving authority to Bush...Then there's an assassination attempt on Reagan and he comes back, three days into his hospital stay he signs the order putting George Bush in charge of the machinery."[134]

Of course, the assassination attempt was not successful in killing the President, and H. W. would have to wait for another chance at the presidency.

First Bush Presidency (George H. W. Bush)
___

During his campaign for the presidency, he famously stated: "*read my lips, no new taxes.*" That was a complete lie and he knew it, but he was willing to do anything and say anything to get elected.[135]

Now President, Bush could look back and know that *"even though he had lied in the face of overwhelming contrary evidence, ignored national and international law, subverted democracy, interfered in the free will of freely elected official foreign governments, allowed known drug traffickers to operate without fear, allowed the importation of drugs into our own country while campaigning a hard line against drugs, and sent American troops into wars as if they were his own personal fighting force,"*[136] all to increase his net worth and consolidate more power, he was still President.

Avoiding the trap of the Iran-Contra scandal, President Bush brought Dick Cheney up from Congress and into the White House as his Secretary of Defense. When Cheney was a Congressman, he had helped (then) VP Bush by authoring a report saying the attempt to give Congress a major role in foreign affairs undermined the presidency.[137] Thus, removing pressure off of the Reagan administration and helped to prevent VP Bush from getting entangled in it.

While writing this book, former President Bush passed away on Saturday, December 1, 2018. With his passing, slowly over the coming years, we might learn more details about the depth of his involvement in many of America's various wars over the past half-century.

The Second Bush President (George W. Bush)

'Dubya' or just 'W.' as he was nicknamed in the media, George W. Bush was a lackluster student in college, earning an average of C-, a lousy pilot in the Texas Air National Guard, and a failing Texas oilman. He was the least capable, least articulate, least prepared individual to ever sit in the Oval Office. And yet, somehow, he became the 46th Governor of Texas, and the 43rd President of the United States.

After college, W. formed an oil exploration company called Arbusto Energy. Financed by his father George H. W., the brother of Osama bin Laden, Salem bin Laden,[138] and a wealthy corrupt banker charged with soliciting deposits from large-scale money laundering and drug dealers, James Bath,[139] W. set out to explore the oil industry. Knowing the Bush family as we do, it should not come as a surprise that W. would form a business with a drug money launderer, but the brother of Osama bin Laden that takes the cake.

Even with the $4.7 million invested and the Bush family name attached to Arbusto, W. quickly ran the company into the ground. Over the coming years, W. would rename the company three times, each in a desperate effort to "rebrand" the company and clear the slate of his previous failures. Cashing in on his family name, he finally settled on the name, "Bush Exploration." With this new name, he was able to convince new investors to invest an additional $7 million. As the *Observer* so eloquently put it, *"whenever he's struck a dry well, someone has always been willing to fill it with money for him."*[140] Yet, even with that influx of cash, the company was strapped and looking for help. A Bush family friend, and owner of Spectrum 7 Energy, came to the rescue and purchased/merged with Bush Exploration.

Coming on the heels of the dot-com boom and bust during the Clinton administration, the economy was already on shaky ground when W. entered office. Then came the events of 9/11. Of course, we have already covered 9/11 in detail, but now, we will highlight a few Bush-related aspects of the 9/11 attacks.

President Bush was in his first year of office as the 43rd President of the United States when the 9/11 attacks took place. What readers may not know is that within the first few days of the Bush administration, there were already talks as to what it would take to invade Iraq and topple the Saddam Hussein regime.[141]

During his administration, Bush not only failed to prevent the 9/11 attacks, but he also ushered in unprecedented violations of citizens' constitutional rights, wasted trillions of U. S. dollars, and countless American lives in the 'War on Terror.'

On the morning of September 11th, President Bush was in Sarasota, Florida at a pre-scheduled photo op at a local elementary school.[142] Prior to walking into the room with the students at 8:55am EST (the same local time as New York and Washington DC), the president was informed that a plane had hit the World Trade Center.[143] At the time, he was informed that it was merely a single plane and there was no need for concern, so the president continued on with his engagement with students. About ten minutes later at 9:05 AM, while in the classroom with students and live on TV, Chief of Staff Andrew Card whispered into Bush's ear *"a second plane hit the second tower. America is under attack."*[144] For reasons only known by the president, he chose to remain in the classroom with the students for just shy of ten minutes,[145] made a quick statement to the nation, and was escorted out of the school by Secret Service at 9:35am.[146]

The St. Petersburg Times asked, *"why [didn't] the Secret Service immediately hustle Bush to a secure location?"*[147] A similar question was asked by the Family Steering Committee: *"Why was President*

Bush permitted by the Secret Service to remain in the Sarasota elementary school where he was reading to children?"[148] Was the Secret Service afraid to overrule the president and force him to leave the school? Or did the Secret Service think the security threat was isolated to New York at that time?

Many conspiracy theories point to the fact that the Secret Service *allowing* him to stay was proof they knew the targets of the attacks beforehand, and already knew that the school was safe. I find this line of *thinking,* if you can even call it that, baseless conjecture without any evidence to support such a statement. Remember, this is still 20-30 minutes before the Pentagon attack, so it is reasonable to believe that the Secret Service did not perceive an immediate threat to the safety of the president as he was located in Florida, not New York.

Some reporters that were at the school commented that Bush appeared lost in thought and stayed in the room longer than he needed to. He did *"excu[se] himself very politely to the teacher and the students,"* as claimed by his Chief of Staff.[149] The media portrayed him as *"openly stretching out the moment,"* and that he *"lingered until the press was gone,"* with Washington Times White House correspondent Bill Sammon referring to the President as the *"dawdler in chief."*[150]

Some theories place the explanation of the emotional response of the President as remorse for his prior knowledge of these attacks, and that he was just biding his time until the full attack was complete. I, however, am not so sure. I think it may be more likely that he was feeling overwhelmed with the sudden realization that he is the one in charge, the one that everyone will look to for guidance, and he knew that he was not up to the challenge. If he could just ignore it, maybe it would go away?

While not degrading the loss of life on 9/11, allow me to provide a very simplistic, yet still applicable comparison. One of the first critical EMS calls I responded to as a certified Paramedic, I looked around hoping someone else would take charge, but everyone was looking at me. I was the Paramedic; I was the one that was there to *save the day*. the EMTs and Police Officers looked to me to provide direction and guidance. I was the one in charge, and on that first call, it took me a few seconds to realize that I must act to save this person's life.

I think it might have been similar for President Bush, because he knew at that very moment that his presidency would be judged solely on his actions and reactions to 9/11. Nothing that he had campaigned on mattered anymore, this was the only issue that America cared about.

Bush-Cheney Administration After The 9/11 Attacks

"In response to the terrorist attacks on September 11, 2001, George W. Bush shredded the US Constitution, trampled on the Bill of Rights, discarded the Geneva Conventions, and helped scorn on the domestic torture statute . . . [I]n response to the attacks, the Bush administration engineered and presided over the most sustained period of constitutional decay in our history" [151]

Not only did the neo-con agenda of total information control over the American people take place, but through their world domination plans, they systematically destroyed the Middle East.

Of course, no one is claiming that the Middle East was a paradise run by saints. However, it was mostly functional, and the dictators in the area mostly kept to themselves and caused little problems for the U.S. directly.

Former State Department employee, Peter Van Buren, summed up his thoughts on the status of the Middle East, and postulated what it would have been like there today if we had not invaded:

> *"Libya was stable, ruled by the same strongman for 42 years; in Egypt, Hosni Mubarak had been in power since 1983; Syria had been run by the Assad family since 1971; Saddam Hussein had essentially been in charge of Iraq since 1969, formally becoming president in 1979; the Turks and Kurds had an uneasy, but functional ceasefire; and Yemen was quiet enough, other than the terror attack on the USS Cole in 2000."*

> *He continued:*

> *"Today Libya is a failed state, bleeding mayhem into Northern Africa; Egypt failed its Arab Spring test and relies on the United States to support is anti-democratic militarized government, and Yemen is a disastrously failed state."[152]*

An astute reader will notice that this is the first section that lists the VP's name in the headline, and this is very befitting of the situation. Dick Cheney was by far the most powerful VP this country has ever seen, and by many accounts, he was the person with the real power and served as the pseudo-President.[153] You may also remember that during the first Bush administration,

Cheney was the Secretary of Defense, and used doctored satellite photos as his primary justification to invade Iraq.[154] Both of these wars were effectively Cheney's wars; he spearheaded them, and cheered for them, and sadly for America, both of the Bush administrations followed his direction.

What did Cheney and the neo-cons gain by attacking Afghanistan and Iraq? First and most importantly, it was justification for increasing their defense spending, not just to U. S. military departments, but countless defense contractors with billions of dollars in contracts each. Secondly, it cleared opposition for an oil and gas pipeline from the Caspian Sea through Afghanistan and Pakistan to the Indian Ocean.[155] The people that control this region of the world stand to earn billions of dollars in oil profits.

As we covered previously in this book, the U.S. government was supporting the Taliban in the mid-90s. However, by the late 90s, the Clinton administration had largely given up on the Taliban.[156]

When Bush-Cheney took office, it gave the Taliban leaders one last chance during a four-day meeting in Berlin in July 2001.[157] An ultimatum was given to the Taliban, *either you accept our offer of a carpet of gold, or we bury you under a carpet of bombs.*[158] As you probably guessed, the Taliban refused this offer and the Bush-Cheney administration replied with *military action against Afghanistan would go ahead . . . before snows start falling in Afghanistan, by the middle of October at the latest.*[159] With the 9/11 attacks, military action took place against Afghanistan on October 7, 2001.

Paul Wolfowitz is quoted as telling the 9/11 Commission that *"it can take a tragedy like September 11th to awaken the world to new threats and to the need for action,"*[160] both he and Donald Rumsfeld agreed that without 9/11, the President would have been unable to convince Congress to *"invade Afghanistan and overthrow the Taliban."*[161]

British Prime Minister Tony Blair said something very similar:

> *"To be truthful about it, there was no way we could have got the public consent to have suddenly launched a campaign on Afghanistan, but for what happened on September 11."*[162]

Of course, none of the above quotes prove that these individuals were in on a conspiracy to allow 9/11 to take place. However, at a minimum, they were knowingly taking advantage of the situation to further their own imperialistic and personal economic goals without giving a damn about the soldiers they were sending to die.

THE CLINTON CRIME FAMILY

William "Bill" and Hillary Clinton rose to power starting with Bill's first run at elected office when he held the position of Attorney General of Arkansas from Jan 3, 1977 - January 9, 1979, and through his ascension through various offices, he eventually became the 42nd President of the United States in 1993. Going along with Bill on his ride to the White House was a very astute lawyer, his wife, Hillary. She would occupy various positions, including First Lady of Arkansas, First Lady of the United States, U.S. Senator for New York, U.S. Secretary of State, and the Democratic Party nominee for President in the 2016 election.

Even to the most casual onlookers, Hillary is the brains of the relationship; Bill had many talents in his own right, including a fantastic ability for charisma. However, it was Hillary's cunningness, drive, and ambition that propelled them both to the White House. A skill Hillary does not possess is likeability. Basically everyone, even those in her party, dislike her personally. She is just not the type of person that people genuinely like. Even Bill had less than favorable views of his wife, often referring to her as "The Warden"[163] or "Hilla the Hun."[164]

Coming To Power

After being recruited into the CIA and graduating from Yale Law School, Bill and Hillary moved to Bill's home state of

Arkansas. Bill immediately entered politics. After losing a race for U.S. Senate, he became the State's Attorney General, and followed this up with a successful bid for Arkansas Governor.

Once Governor, Bill and Hillary immediately looked at how to use their power and influence to benefit themselves personally. She invested $1,000 in cattle futures and walked away with $99,537 in about 1-year.[165] This seeming impossible feat of investment prowess was compared to *"had Hillary instead invested $1,000 in the first offering of Microsoft stock in 1986, she would have made $25,835 by March 1994."*[166]

One might consider it beginners luck, as Hillary so eloquently put it whenever she was questioned about it. However, after some investigative journalists dug into the story a little more, they discovered that Hillary did not purchase the cattle futures directly, no. Instead, she had an associate purchase them on her behalf. That is not a crime; remember, this was long before eTrade online. What is interesting though, is that the person that purchased the futures for her, Jim Blair, was the head legal counsel for Tyson Foods;[167] the same Tyson Foods that was currently in legal trouble for having poultry processing plants that dumped *"tons of chicken feces into nearby Dry Creek."*[168] After Hillary *earned* the $100k, Tyson was awarded $8 million in tax concessions, relaxation of environmental regulations,[169] and $900k in state grant money to build roads into their plant.[170]

This wouldn't be the only time the Clintons received financial benefits from Tyson Foods and/or their owner Don Tyson. The FBI investigated allegations by Tyson employee, Joseph Hendrickson, who delivered envelopes with *"quarter-inch [thick with] $100 bills, on six different occasions to the governor's mansion."*

He said the deliveries were for Bill Clinton.[171] Investigators felt that they had enough evidence to charge Bill for bribery, however, the investigations were shut down by the upper echelons of the Arkansas State Police.[172]

How did the Clintons get away with this? It was simple, Bill stacked the deck in his favor by appointing as many of his hand-picked cronies as possible to every high ranking position in the government. This is something he would repeat as President, and *"quietly fired every U.S. Attorney in the country and then made his move on the FBI, which would be a replica of the Arkansas State Police."*[173]

Rebuilding the U. S. Justice Department and the FBI would serve the Clintons many times over as they systematically and carefully overlooked numerous crimes and various scandals that the Clintons would be a part of for decades to come.

Dr. Paul Fick wrote a psychological analysis of Bill:

> *"He had a rollercoaster candidacy with many highs and potential campaign destroying lows; he was faced with repeated embarrassing disclosures about his personal life; he responded to these disclosures with a glaring tendency to lie; he appeared indecisive and waffled on significant issues, and he was energized by the self-created chaos."*[174]

Author Victor Thorn summarizes Hillary's corruption this way:

> *"Hillary Clinton has been directly involved in nearly every major scandal of the last thirty years, including Watergate, Whitewater Iran-Contra, Inslaw and*

PROMIS, the BCCI banking debacle, the disastrous S&L bailouts, drug trafficking in Mena while her husband was governor of Arkansas, Travelgate, Filegate, Waco, the murders of Vince Foster and Ron Brown, OKC, and the shootdown of flight 800."[175]

Guns-for-Drugs Operation

At the end of the Iran-Contra saga, and more specifically the Guns-for-Drugs operation, Vice President Bush directed CIA operations aimed at trading US weapons for cocaine and marijuana with the Contras. The drugs were flying in 24/7 to a small airport in Mena, Arkansas, which became the base of the single largest cocaine smuggling operation in U.S. History[176]. Sworn testimony from Chip Tatum, a pilot for the CIA's "Pegasus" project, recalled a conversation between him and Oliver North during a flight where North stated, *"One more year of this and we'll retire."* This was followed up with remarks about Barry Seal [*pilot that claimed he possessed evidence against Jeb Bush and was murdered in Miami*] and Governor Clinton, *"If we can keep those Arkansas hicks in line, that is."*[177]

"Bill Clinton and his circle of friends lived above the law and gained access to rivers of dirty [CIA drug] money in exchange for little more than keeping their mouths shut and staying out of the way."[178]

Clinton's direct knowledge of the drug flow is unquestionable. In 1988, Chuck Black the assistant prosecutor for Polk County, told Gov. Clinton:

> *"We know what's going down here. We know about tons of cocaine and tons of weapons and hundreds of millions of dollars going through the local bank.*

We know about hundreds of people who have been trained here at Mena."[179]

Rather than dedicate resources to assist the ADA with investigating the drugs coming into Mena, Gov. Clinton smashed the investigation, and later, Arkansas Committee leader Tom Brown would recount a meeting with Gov. Clinton:

> *"Clinton told us he knew about the CIA, knew about Bush, and knew about the drugs, but for some reason, we never heard anything more about it."[180]*

Why would Gov. Clinton allow this, aside for the obvious fact of the money paid to him? Simple, he was just following orders from his CIA handlers. *"George Bush [was] in the direct chain of command"*[181] and Bill and Hillary were just puppets in a much larger show, *"understand that [Bill] Clinton is not the brilliant crook. It's just that he followed orders."*[182]

CIA Agent William Barr, who later was appointed U.S. Attorney General by George Bush, was quoted screaming to Gov. Clinton during a meeting:

> *"Our deal was for you to get 10% of the profits, not 10% of the gross. This has turned into a feeding frenzy by your good-ole-boy sharks and you've had a hand in it too, Mr. Clinton. Just ask your Mr. Nash to produce a business card. I'll bet it reads Arkansas Development and Finance Authority. This ADFA of yours is double-dipping. Our deal with you was to launder our money. You get 10% after costs and post-tax profits. No one agreed for you to start loaning out money to your friends through your ADFA so that they*

could buy machinery to build our guns. That wasn't the deal. Mr. Sawahata tells me that one of ADFA's first customers was some parking meter company that got several million dollars in ... how shall we say it. .. in preferred loans...Dammit, we bought a whole gun company, lock, stock, and barrel and shipped the whole thing down here for you. And Mr. Reed even helped set it up. You people go and screw us by setting up some subcontractors that weren't even authorized by us. ****, people who didn't even have security clearances. That's why we're pulling the operation out of Arkansas. It's become a liability for us. We don't need alive liabilities."[183]

Even with mountains of demonstrable evidence that *tons* of illegal drugs were being imported into Mena, and billions of dollars in illicit drug money were being laundered through local Arkansas banks, *"not a single major bust was ever made out of Arkansas, out of Mena"*.[184] In fact, *"officials repeatedly involved national security to quash most of the investigations."*[185] As time went on, it became *"apparent that Mena enjoyed a special status. Every attempt to investigate was met with inference. Investigator Russell Welch of the Arkansas Police was ordered to stay away from the drug activity at the Mena Airport."*[186]

"By the end of 1987, thousands of law enforcement man-hours and an enormous amount of evidence of drug smuggling, aiding and abetting drug smugglers, conspiracy, perjury, [and] money laundering had gone to waste. Not only were no indictments ever returned on any of the individuals under investigation for their

role in the Mena operation, there was a complete breakdown in the judicial system. The United States Attorney, Western Judicial District of Arkansas refused to issue subpoenas for critical witnesses, interfered in the investigations, misled grand juries about evidence and availability of the witnesses, refused to allow investigators to present evidence to the grand jury, and in general made a mockery of the inter investigative and judicial process.[187]

"During the 1980s, as much as $100 million a month in cocaine had been flown into the airport at Mena and much of that money had been laundered through ADFA, a bonding agency Governor Clinton had created to help small businesses get started."[188]

There is little doubt that the ADFA was little more than a *"wholly-controlled financial entity for laundering large sums of cocaine money from Mena,"*[189] with *"upwards of $18 billion [passing] through ADFA between 1985 and 1992."*[190]

Where did all this money go? Back into the hands of the criminal conspirators, of course. In December of 1988, the ADFA raised $50 million to build homes for the poor. Instead, the $50 million was wired to Fuji Bank, Grand Cayman Branch, account #63119808.[191] Why else would money be sent to the Cayman Islands, except for drug smuggling? Last I checked, Home Depot and Lowes do not have you wire money to offshore financial havens when you order lumber.

Of course, an astute reader might say to themselves, *"but these bonds are loans and must be paid back."* In reality, no, they were purposefully designed to not be paid back and were simply, *"being zeroed out - as though payments were being made - when in fact no payments of any kind were being made."*[192] This is a typical Ponzi scheme; as long as deposits keep coming in from laundering drug money, the accounting books can be cooked.

To add insult to injury, after seasoning the loans for a year or two, the ADFA would package these junk bonds along with good bonds and sell them off to various banks. Former ADFA marketing director Larry Nichols, claims:

> *"that no one was actually buying these bonds; that they were instead sold to out-of-state banks, two with connections to [international drug money laundering bank] BCCI. The losses from these junk bonds were then mixed into the vortex of vanishing money in the S&L [Savings & Loans] crisis".* [193]

If that wasn't bad enough, every bond issued by ADFA had the loan documents executed at the same law firm that Hillary worked for, the Rose Law Firm.[194]

Whitewater Scandal

While the drugs and ADFA scams were not very well known to the public, it was not long into their political careers that the Clintons were embroidered in widespread public scandals. One of the most notorious at the time was the Whitewater Scandal. Not much of the formal details were ever released to the public; because the media chose to repeat Hillary's words and portray it as simply a failed business venture, instead of the fraud that it truly was.

What we do know is, a real estate investment company by the name of Whitewater Developer Corporation was formed in 1979 by Bill & Hillary Clinton[195] and Jim & Susan McDougal. At the time, Bill was transitioning from Attorney General of Arkansas to the Governor of Arkansas. Hillary was working for a legal firm that would represent Whitewater, Jim was running Madison Guaranty Savings and Loan, and lastly, Susan was an aide to Bill Clinton.

It is alleged that the Clintons fraudulently encouraged Jim's bank to illegally issue numerous loans both to the Clintons and to straw buyers to help prop up the failing Whitewater Development Corp[196].

Many decades later, a non-profit organization called Judicial Watch was able to obtain the notes of federal prosecutors investigating the Whitewater scandal via a Freedom of Information Act request:

> *"Several pieces of evidence support the inference that personal documents which Hillary Clinton did not want disclosed were located in (Clinton personal lawyer Vince) Foster's office at the time of his death and then removed."*

> *"That evening and the next morning, White House counsel Bernie Nussbaum, Hillary Clinton, Susan Thomases, and Maggie Williams, Hillary Clinton's chief of staff, exchanged 10 separate phones calls. That morning, according to Department of Justice employees, Nussbaum changed his mind, and refused to allow the prosecutors to review the documents.*

Instead, he reviewed them himself, and designated several as 'personal' to the Clintons."

"On the evening of July 22, 1993, Thomas Castleton . . . assisted Williams in carrying a box of personal documents up to . . . a closet in Hillary Clinton's office. The closet is approximately 30 feet from the table in the Book Room, where the billing records were found two years later. . . . There is a circumstantial case that the records were left on the table by Hillary Clinton. She is the only individual in the White House who had a significant interest in them and she is one of only three people known to have had them in her possession since their creation in February 1992."

The prosecutors never filed for an indictment of the Clintons because they felt they had less than a 10% chance of convicting Hillary for her actions. They contend that the evidence was substantial enough to indicate that she most likely knew about the illegal activities. However, they did not have enough evidence to prove that she actively participated in said illegal actions. The evidence they suspected to exist mysteriously disappeared, and Hillary is the last person known to have the items in her possession.

In the end, many persons surrounding the Clintons, including one of Hillary's law partners, Webster Hubbell, were convicted for various crimes including embezzlement, concealment of funds, fraud, and other financial crimes. In addition to Webster, fifteen others were convicted of more than 40 crimes.[197] Four of these individuals convicted, all close Clinton aides, were later pardoned by President Clinton[198].

Vince Foster, a lawyer and *"Hillary Clinton's closest friend, the one person in the world that she would entrust with the most sensitive problems"*[199] was found dead in an overgrown and obscure park in Washington DC. The full story of his death could take up an entire book, or even a series of books, to fully cover all of the details of this complex subject. I invite you to read *Hillary (and Bill) The Murder Volume: Part Three of the Clinton Trilogy by Victor Thorn,* as he gives a much more detailed account than I can do justice to in this section.

The official government story read that Vince was depressed and took his own life. In fact, it was a shotty and ill-planned murder that if not for the political power of the First Lady, even the most junior detective in the country would have solved the case before breakfast.

So, why was Vince murdered? Was it Hillary that ordered it? While he knew a lot of dirt on the Clinton's, they knew he was a staunch supporter and advocate of theirs. Additionally, the details of the cover-up were very 'last-minute' and any murder ordered by the Clintons would have allowed for more time to plan a cover-up. So if it was not Hillary, then who killed Vince? In one word, "the Mossad."

The Mossad is Israel's version of the United States' NSA. *"In Arkansas, the Mossad is said to have found out about Vince Foster's payoff role in the illegal CIA-backed drugs-and-guns-and-money in Mena operation, and so the Israelis blackmailed Foster for information on FOBs (Friends of Bill Clinton - who by this time had made it to the White House)."* [200]

According to insiders, the details of his arrangement with the Mossad included:

> *"Foster was to leak codes and secrets to the Israelis in exchange for their promise to not expose him, his connections with drug running, and money laundering for Clinton, and in addition, the Israelis would add to his Swiss bank account - which they had already discovered by means of their very special computer software [PROMIS] given [stolen] to them by someone in the U.S. government."*[201]

The PROMIS software was rumored to be stolen by the U.S. and given to the Mossad using the information provided by Foster.

At the time of his death, he was in some serious trouble as *"the CIA had Foster under serious investigation for leaking hi-security secrets to the State of Israel."*[202] In the weeks leading up to his death, Vince began writing down details and collecting evidence of his actions on behalf of Israel, so that he could turn state's evidence and seek immunity for his actions. This is corroborated by his wife during her interviews with investigators.

On the day of his death, by all outward appearances, Vince was acting normal and did not give any indications that he was suicidal. Of course, as a career liar and manipulator of facts, it is very possible that he was able to fool even those around him. However, these statements by his co-workers aside, the actual facts of the case point strictly to murder and coverup.

The last two people to officially see Vince alive were Linda Tripp when around *"one pm on July 20, 1993, Foster stopped by Tripp's desk, lifted some M&Ms from a bowl and said, 'I'll be back.'*

He never returned."[203] and Secret Service officer John Skyles as he was guarding the gate Foster exited shortly after 1pm[204]. He would later testify before the Senate that *"Foster did not appear to be at all depressed or preoccupied as he walked by."*[205]

Interestingly, while the Secret Service has a log entry of Foster walking out of the White House, there is no entry of him driving his vehicle out of the parking lot that afternoon. There is an entry of him parking his vehicle in the morning, but no log entry nor video surveillance tapes of him driving off. Yet his vehicle somehow manages to leave the secured parking garage, travel across town, and ends up in a parking lot adjacent to the park where his body is found hours later. How is it possible that someone can be 'missed' by the Secret Service coming and going from one of the most secure buildings in the world? Either the officer should have been fired for incompetence, or more likely, someone with significant power was able to make the log entry and videotapes disappear.

Back in Little Rock, Arkansas; on the day of the murder at around 4:48 pm CST (5:48 pm EST), Trooper Larry Patterson received a phone call, *"It was [Trooper] Roger Perry. He said that he just received a call from Helen Dickey [White House aide and former nanny of Chelsea] that Vince Foster had blown his brains out in the parking lot of the White House."*[206] This phone call took place approximately 30 mins before Park Police first found Vince's body at Fort Marcy Park and at that time they had yet to identify who the person was.

Yes, you read this correctly. White House staff called a friend back in Arkansas saying Vince had killed himself in the White House parking lot, yet the official location where his body was discovered was in a park some 20 minutes away. To top it off, this phone call occurred 30 minutes prior to the discovery of Vince's body, and nearly four hours before the White House was officially notified by Park Police of Foster's death.

Both Troopers Perry and Patterson were interviewed and each confirmed the timeline of sometime between approximately 4:45-4:48 pm when the phone call took place. They also stated that they felt as though the FBI agent interviewing them was attempting to convince them to *"change my story"* to get the timeline to match with the White House's official story.[207]

Vince Foster's body was found at 6:14 pm EST (5:15 pm CST) by U.S. Park Police deep inside the wooded Fort Marcy Park, which is best described as a *'deserted park.'*[208] According to the officers on-scene, the body was found lying supine with arms

Date	Aircraft Make and Model	Aircraft Identification Mark	Points of Departure & Arrival		Miles Flown	Flight Hrs	Remarks, Procedures, Maneuvers, Endorsements	Number of Landings	Aircraft Categ	
			From	To						NSRPA. 6
15	B-727-31	N908JC	LGA	BED		47	JC	1/1		7
15	''	''	BED	HPN		48	JC, JESSICA			8
17	''	''	HPN	TEST		49	JC,GM,SK,M,CINDY LUBER,		3 4
20	''	''	TEST	PBI		50	JC,GM,SK,JM,CINDY LOPER JOHNNY	1/1	2 6
22	''	''	PBI	HPN		51	JC,GM,SK,JM,CINDY LUBER	1/	2 5
25	''	''	HPN	PBI		52	JC,GM,SK,JM AUSTIN PINTO		2 7
27	''	''	PBI	TEST		53	JC,GM,SK,JM TUTTLE, MAUI,	1/	2 4
30	''	''	TEST	JFK		54	JC,GM,SK,JM,JM TUTTLE,CINDY LUBER	1/	3 7
3	''	''	JFK	PBI		55	JC			
9	''	''	PBI	MIA		57	BILL CLINTON, 4 SECRET SERVICE 2 MALES, 1 FEMALE JC GM SK, JM			
10	''	''	MIA	HPN		58	JC,GM,SK,JM, FLEUR PERRY JM			
13	''	''	HPN	LFPB						
14	''	''	LFPB	LIML		60	JC,SK	1/	4 4
15	''	''	LIML	EGGW		61	JC,SK	1/	2 4
15	''	''	EGGW	BGR		62	JC,GM,SK		1 8
16	''	''	BGR	PBI		63	JC,GM,SK	2	7 2
18	G-1159	N9C4TC	PBI	ADY		65	JC	1/1	3 5
18	''	''	ADY	PBI		66	EMPTY	1/1	1 4
								1 1	
							Page Total	12	51 0

neatly by his sides, palms up, with no weapon found by the body. *"A .38 caliber revolver was found in the car."*[209]

Sgt. George Gonzalez, U.S. Park Police was the first officer to discover Foster's body and he insisted under questioning by the FBI that there had been no gun near or on the body, or in either hand.[210] Two other witnesses including Sgt John Rolla, stated that there was no gun in Foster's hands when they arrived and that "*the palms were up.*"[211]

According to the official story, Vince parked his car [yes the same car that "magically left" the White House parking lot] and walked 700 plus feet through highly-grown summer vegetation, yet miraculously, "*the FBI lab found not a speck of soil on his shoes or clothing. No grass stains were mentioned. No soil -- yet almost every garment of clothing, including his underwear, was covered in multi-colored carpet fibers.*"[212] Obviously this man missed his calling in life, he should not have been a high-priced lawyer, he should have been a magician. Not only did he make his car disappear from a secure White House parking lot and reappear in a park, but he also managed to levitate his body through 700 feet of wooded terrain without a single piece of grass or dirt attaching to his clothing.

"*Beyond belief, when official reports were released, they stated the gun which Vince Foster supposedly used to kill himself was still in his hand upon death.*"[213] The official report even included a photograph of Vince with a gun in his hand. Yet the sworn testimony of the officers on the scene all say that the gun was located in his vehicle, not his hand. The gun that was later claimed to be in his hand, was discovered to have no fingerprints from Foster, nor any blood.[214]

The medical examiner observed a *"small caliber bullet hole on the ride side of Foster's neck, possibly a .22 caliber,"*[215] which is inconsistent with the .38 reported to be found in Foster's hand.

The truth is that Foster was murdered in the parking lot of the White House, by Mossad agents fearful that Vince was about to tell the truth about Israeli involvement in the theft of U.S. government secrets. They killed him, and left his body for Hillary to deal with. They knew that if Foster was 'murdered,' she would be the first to get blamed. Hillary then went into a panicked 'fixer' mode; she had his body wrapped up in carpet, which explains the carpet fibers on his body, moved out to the park, and tried to cover the tracks and stage it as a suicide.

Within hours of Foster's death, Hillary's team had the Secret Service's Maintenance and Installation Group, break into Foster's White House safe and quickly clear out most of the files in his office. Why would Hillary do this? To prevent the FBI or Park Police from accidentally finding incriminating evidence against the Clintons that Vince may or may not have saved?

Sexual Misdeeds

Many intelligent men in the past have had various forms of addiction, either drugs or alcohol. *"Everyone you think he fucked, he did -- and the more dangerous the better . . . His addiction is pussy."*[216]

In 1999, Capitol Hill Blue published a scathing report saying *"Juanita isn't the only one: Bill Clinton's long history of sexual violence against women dates back some 30 years."* [217] This, of course, was referring to Juanita Broaddrick, a former nursing home administrator who alleged that Clinton raped her in a hotel room and had the Arkansas State Police cover it up in the 1970s.

Bill's history of sexual interactions with females is questionable at best, and at worst, outright forcible rape. He has been accused of:

- Raping Juanita Broaddrick when he served as Arkansas Attorney General in 1978[218]

- Sexual assaulting Leslie Milwee in 1980[219]

- Forcibly groping Kathleen Willey and forcing her hand upon his erect penis without her permission in 1993[220]

- Forcing the former Miss Arkansas, Elizabeth Ward Gracen to have sex with him against her will in 1983 when she, in tears, *"described Clinton pushing himself on her as she pleaded that she did not want to have sex"*[221]

- Exposing himself to Paula Jones multiple times between 1998-1999[222]

These are just a few of the women that publicly accused Bill of rape or sexual misconduct against their will. This does not even touch the ones that were paid to keep quiet, nor does it cover the ones that had consensual adulterous sexual relations with Bill while he was married. Personally, I do not care what consenting adults do behind closed doors, it is not my business if he cheated on Hillary and is not the business of anyone else. What does concern me, however, is Bill's reported abuse of power both in the use of government resources for personal gain and covering up rape. Case in point when it can be said that, *"nearly a dozen Arkansas state police troopers were used as pimps in uniform to feed their boss's insatiable sexual appetite."*[223]

"We were required to work overtime so we could sit outside some place and block the road or sit in some driveway or apartment complex while he went in to take care of his female friends. . . State money was utilized." Arkansas State Trooper, Larry Patterson.[224]

This is the big difference between Bill's sexual activities and that of current President Donald Trump. Bill abused his power to subvert justice when he raped multiple women and converted government funds to pay for state troopers to act as pimps, whereas Trump had consensual sex with models, paid them to keep quiet and lied about it to his wife. There are no rape accusations against Trump, just an old billionaire that fucked some hot models; who cares?

At first, Clinton would bribe his victims to keep quiet, but if that didn't work, he would have his thugs make threatening phone calls telling them to *"keep your mouth shut about Bill Clinton and go on with your life."[225]* If the initial phone calls did not send the message, the IRS would then issue audits and threats, which was reported by at least four of his victims including Gennifer Flowers, Paula Jones, Juanita Broaddrick, and Elizabeth Gracen, who all said that receiving threats by the IRS.[226]

Hillary was also a willing co-conspirator in Bill's sexually deviant acts, choosing the path of political power rather than allow the public truth of Bill's most illicit activities to come to light. She knew it would be the end of both of their political careers if Bill was found guilty of rape and adultery. For this reason, *"Hillary hired private detectives to identify the women her husband was sleeping with [and raping], and to intimidate these women, so that they would not go public with their stories.*"[227] So much for Hillary being a champion for women's rights.

The Clinton Campaign paid private investigator Anthony Pellicano $100,000 in "*legal fees*"[228] to prevent women from "*going public with accusations that Bill Clinton had bedded, raped, impregnated, sexually assaulted, or otherwise used and abused them.*"[229] But do not just take my word for it, let's read Pellicano's own words from an interview included in the January 1992 issue of *GQ Magazine*: "*I'm an expert with a knife...I can shred your face with a knife.*"[230] What legitimate reason would the Clinton's have for a thug like that on the payroll, and why would it be listed as "legal fees"?

After the election, White House Chief of Staff Betsey Wright reportedly kept Pellicano on the payroll to keep a lid on Bill Clinton's "*bimbo eruptions.*"[231]

Jeffrey Epstein

Bill's misdeeds are not limited to the women we already know about; he has been rumored to have engaged in sex with underage girls on the private Boeing 727 jet of convicted pedophile and registered sex offender, Jeffrey Epstein. His jet was often referred to in the media as the "Lolita Express." Flight logs obtained from the Federal Aviation Administration (FAA) by Gawker[232] in January of 2015 put former President Clinton:

> "*[on the] billionaire's infamous jet more than a dozen times sometimes with a woman whom federal prosecutors suspect of procuring underage sex victims for Mr. Epstein.*"[233]

During at least five of these flights with Epstein, Clinton turned down Secret Service escort and protection.[234] This is a claim that Secret Service will not confirm nor deny officially. Bill has flown on Epstein's private jet at least 26 times.[235]

"Bill Clinton ... associated with a man like Jeffrey Epstein, who everyone in New York, certainly within his inner circles, knew was a pedophile," said Conchita Sarnoff, of the Washington, D.C.-based non-profit, Alliance to Rescue Victims of Trafficking. *"Why would a former president associate with a man like that?"*

In 2005, Palm Beach Police investigated Epstein for over a year after the parents of a 14-year-old girl alleged their daughter was lured into Epstein's mansion, paid $300 to strip to her underwear and massage Epstein[236]. Police interviewed dozens of witnesses, confiscated his trash, performed surveillance, and searched his Palm Beach mansion. During their search, police found large numbers of photos of nude and semi-nude underage girls throughout the house, some of whom the police had interviewed in the course of their investigation.[237] At the conclusion of their investigation, they had identified 20 girls between the ages of 14 and 17 who they said were sexually abused by Epstein.[238]

In 2006, the FBI was brought in to assist local police and launched their own probe into allegations that Epstein and his personal assistants had *"used facilities of interstate commerce to induce girls between the ages of 14 and 17 to engage in illegal sexual activities."*[239]

According to court documents, police investigators found a *"clear indication that Epstein's staff was frequently working to schedule multiple young girls between the ages of 12 and 16 years old literally every day, often two or three times per day."*

The U.S. Attorney for the Southern District of Florida prepared to charge Epstein for child sex abuse, witness tampering, and money laundering, but Epstein was tipped off and plead guilty to just one count of soliciting prostitution from an underage girl under Florida state law before an indictment could be handed up.

Bush's Attorney General Alberto Gonzales, told the *Daily Beast* that he *"instructed the Justice Department to pursue justice without making a political mess."*[240] This is basically all you need to know about the case; Clinton's friends are protected at all costs. It does not matter if they were Republicans or Democrats; it is, quite simply, one Deep State of corruption.

On September 24, 2007, in a deal shrouded in secrecy that left alleged victims shocked at its leniency, Epstein agreed to a 30-month sentence, including 18 months of jail time and 12 months of house arrest, along with an agreement to pay dozens of young girls under a federal statute providing for compensation to victims of child sexual abuse. In exchange, the U.S. Attorney's Office promised not to pursue any federal charges against Epstein or his co-conspirators.

It has been rumored that Epstein had beds installed in his private jet, along with hidden cameras to record the sex acts between his wealthy friends and underage boys/girls. If this latter part is true, it would be reasonable to believe that he is in possession of incriminating video evidence against some very powerful people, possibly including the former President.

We are left to wonder just how Epstein was able to get off so light during his sentencing? If the situation was different, and the evidence was against any other person like you or me, you know the jail sentence would have been much stiffer. It is evident to everyone that someone in high power determined that a public trial of Epstein would bring the underage sex activities of Clinton and other politically powerful individuals into the public light. Even if, for the sake of argument, Bill Clinton was not being blackmailed by Epstein, the fact that Epstein was able to bargain down his charges proves that there are two justice systems in this country; one for you and me, and one for the rich and powerful.

Clinton Foundation

The Clinton Foundation was founded in 1997 by Bill Clinton towards the end of his second term as President, and as of 2016, had received more than $2 billion in donations.[241]

Before Bill even left office, the foundation was already embroidered in controversy. In October of 1999, just a month after the Clinton administration's FTC *"dropped a bid to regulate beer, wine, and liquor advertising [targeted to minors]"* Anheuser-Busch donated $1 million to the foundation.[242]

In January of 2009, before Hillary could be confirmed as the Secretary of State for the Obama administration, she sat before the Senate Foreign Relations Committee to answer questions about her involvement in the Clinton Foundation.

> *"The core of the problem is that foreign governments and entities may perceive the Clinton Foundation as a means to gain favor with the Secretary of State,"* Senator Richard Lugar said.[243]

With this controversy hot on their the minds, the Senators required Hillary to sign a Memorandum of Understanding (MOU) that would outline her commitments to transparency regarding certain types of donations received by the Clinton Foundation while she served as Secretary of State.

The notable points included[244]:

- The Clinton Foundation would disclose its contributors: *"... The Foundation will publish its contributors this year. During any service by Senator Clinton as Secretary of State, the Foundation will publish annually the names of contributors."*

- Bill Clinton would not *"personally solicit funds"* for the Clinton Global Initiative (CGI), a subsidiary of the Clinton Foundation, and its annual meeting in New York to address global issues such as poverty, health, and climate change.

- CGI would also not be permitted to accept contributions from foreign governments, except through attendance fees, and it would suspend plans to do international events, such as the one held annually in New York.

- Other subsidiaries, including the Clinton HIV/AIDS Initiative, which hadn't been disclosing donors, would be forced to disclose any new contributors or increased contributions beyond what donors had already been giving: *"... The Foundation will share such countries and the circumstances of the anticipated contribution with the State Department designated agency ethics official for review, and as appropriate, the State Department's designated agency ethics official will submit the matter for review by a designated official in the White House Counsel's Office.*

Between the years of 2009 and 2013, a Russian controlled company purchased Canada-based Uranium One, a company that controls almost one-fifth of all uranium production in America. Due to obvious security ramifications of outside entities having a controlling interest in America's uranium production, the purchase first had to be approved by multiple U.S. government departments and agencies. This included Secretary Clinton's State Department.

At that time, Obama was in complete denial about the looming threat from Russia, but Republicans on the House Foreign Relations Committee expressed opposition to the deal, citing numerous national security concerns.[245] Those concerns would be ignored and the deal was approved. If it were not for the seriousness of the threat, it would almost be humorous in how Democrats flipped from saying that Russia was no threat, to pointing fingers at Evil Trump and his Russian connections.

The New York Times, would investigate the Uranium One deal more than a year and a half before the 2016 election and they concluded:

> *"As the Russians gradually assumed control of Uranium One in three separate transactions from 2009 to 2013, Canadian records show, a flow of cash made its way to the Clinton Foundation. Those contributions were not publicly disclosed by the Clintons, despite an agreement Mrs. Clinton had struck with the Obama White House to publicly identify all donors. Other people with ties to the company made donations as well."[246]*

The facts that we know are that Uranium One's chairman used his family foundation to make four donations totaling $2.35 million to the Clinton Foundation during this time.[247] Shortly after the public announcement of Russian acquisition of Uranium One, Mr. Clinton was paid $500,000 to give a speech in Moscow for Renaissance Capital by the same Russian investment bank that was promoting Uranium One stock.

The Washington Post, a newspaper that had historically been very pro-Clinton found that 1,100 donors to the Clinton Foundation came from close associates of Uranium One and that these donations were kept secret and were never disclosed, as required by Hillary's agreement during her confirmation.[248]

Very little evidence is publicly available prove that the donations played any direct role or not in the approval of the deal. It does, however, bring to light a severe conflict of interest and additional ethical considerations when a former president relies heavily on foreign cash to accumulate a $250+ million in personal assets, while at the same time his wife serves as the country's Secretary of State and helps to steer American foreign policy.

Bill would continue to be paid millions, both personally and with donations to the Foundation for speaking engagements overseas, many of them connected with Hillary's work at the State Department.[249]

During Hillary Clinton's tenure as Secretary of State, many individuals, organizations, and countries allegedly contributed to the Clinton Foundation either before, or while pursuing interests through ordinary channels within the U.S. State Department.[250]

"At least 85 of 154 people from private interests who met or had phone conversations scheduled with Clinton while she led the State Department, donated to her family charity or pledged commitments to its international programs [...] combined, the 85 donors contributed as much as $156 million."[251]

In 2014, the *Washington Post* reported that there was *"substantial overlap between the Clinton political machinery and the Foundation."* They further revealed that nearly half of the major donors who had backed *Ready for Hillary* had also given at least $10,000 to the Foundation. In some cases, it was in the form of personal donations, or through foundations or outside companies.[252] By itself, this may not be a criminal violation of federal law. However, it does raise the possibility of campaign finance reform violations if the donations to the Foundation were made to circumvent campaign finance rules.

In February 2015, *The Washington Post* reported that while Hillary served as Secretary of State, the Clinton Foundation accepted millions of U.S. dollars in donations from at least seven different foreign governments, including a donation of $500,000 from Algeria. This donation was not vetted by the State Department, in direct violation of Clinton's MOU agreement. The *Post* noted that the donation *"coincided with a spike"* in lobbying efforts by Algeria towards the State Department regarding their human rights record.

In November 2016, Reuters reported that:

"The Clinton Foundation has confirmed it accepted a $1 million gift from Qatar while Hillary Clinton was

U.S. Secretary of State without informing the State Department, even though she had promised to let the agency review new or significantly increased support from foreign governments. "[253]

In a closed-door session with Congress, undercover informant William Douglas Campbell testified that Russia routed millions of dollars to an American-based lobbying firm to influence Hillary.[254] He further testified he knows of at least $3 million of the donations were sent to Clinton's Global Initiative at the same time that Russia was seeking approval to purchase Uranium One,[255] along with reports detailing how a Russian official *"boasted about how weak the U.S. Government was in giving away uranium business"*[256]

The Clinton Foundation had officially resumed accepting donations from foreign governments once Secretary Clinton's tenure had ended.[257] It is important to note that any kind of contributions from foreign donors to political candidates is strictly prohibited by law, yet foreign money constitutes a significant portion of the Foundation's income.

In October of 2017, *The Hill* reported that, *"the FBI had gathered substantial evidence that Russian nuclear industry officials were engaged in bribery, kickbacks, extortion, and money laundering designed to grown Vladimir Putin's atomic energy business inside the United States, according to government documents and interviews."*[258]

Does this mean that the Clinton Foundation was a "pay to play" scheme as many believe? While it is hard to prove beyond any reasonable doubt that payments were bribes, it is not as if someone simply wrote a check to the Clinton Foundation with a check memo of "Money to bribe Hillary to do X, Y, and Z for me." Absent of direct evidence as such, we must look at the totality of the evidence as a whole. Payments were made to both Bill personally and the Foundation by multiple international entities, each with a personal interest in foreign relations that Hillary could influence in one way or another. It is also very interesting to note that once Hillary lost the presidential election, the vast sums of money coming into the Foundation all but dried up, showing a 37% drop literally overnight.[259] This, combined with the personal income for paid speeches, went from $3.6 million to only $357,500.[260] Why, you ask? Because no one wants to bribe a politician that is no longer in power. This single fact alone proves to me that the Clinton Foundation and Bill's paid speeches were bribes.

"The Clinton Foundation's downward trajectory ever since Clinton's election loss provides further testimony to claims that the organization was built on greed and the lust for power and wealth--not charity.[261]" wrote Michael Sainato for the Observer.

2012 Terrorist Attack in Benghazi

The horrific attacks that took place in Benghazi, Libya deserve entire books to be written about them. However, for expediency, I will only cover the small aspects that pertain to our subject, Hillary.

On September 11, 2012, at 9:40 pm (Benghazi time), a coordinated attack took place against two U.S. government facilities in Benghazi by Islamic militant terrorists from Ansar al-Sharia. During this attack, U.S. Ambassador to Libya, Christopher Stevens, and three other U.S. nationals were killed.

Hillary initially blamed an internet video posted to YouTube with the title, *Innocence of Muslims,* as the reason for the attack in Benghazi, saying, *"Some have sought to justify this vicious behavior as a response to inflammatory material posted on the Internet."* [262] She would repeat this narrative multiple times. [263] [264] [265]

This lie was picked up by the Obama administration and they continued to run with it, *"We have no information to suggest that is was a pre-planned attack. The unrest we've seen around the region has been in reaction to a video that Muslims, many Muslims find offensive."* [266] The problem for the administration and for Hillary is that we know it was not in response to the video. In fact, it has been confirmed that both Obama and Clinton knew it was a pre-planned attack. CIA Director David Petraeus testified to Congress that the Obama administration knew the attack was an act of terrorism committed by an al-Qaeda-linked group early on. [267]

So, why blame it on a YouTube video, instead of admitting that it was a terrorist attack from an al-Qaeda-linked group? The issue lied in the fact that the administration would have to admit that their removal of Gaddafi had destabilized the region and allowed al-Qaeda to grow in power. This theory is backed up by recently declassified emails, *"showing then-White House Deputy Strategic Communications Adviser Ben Rhodes and other Obama administration public relations officials attempting to orchestrate a campaign to 'reinforce' President Obama and to portray the Benghazi consulate terrorist attack as being 'rooted in an internet video, and not a failure of policy."* [268]

On the same day as the attacks, Hillary emailed her daughter Chelsea and informed her that *"based upon the information we saw today we believe the group that claimed responsibility for this was affiliated with al-Qaeda."*[269] Yet, she continued with the lie about the YouTube video as it was more in line with the narrative that protected her and the Obama administration.

Immediately after the attacks, there were calls for congressional investigations into how and why an ambassador and his security detail were left to die at the embassy. This brings us to the U.S. House Select Committee on Benghazi. During their investigations into what Secretary Clinton knew prior to the attack, they discovered her illegal email server, and this is when the investigation took a dramatic turn. [See Email Scandal]

At the conclusion of their investigation, they would report that safety conditions in Libya were deteriorating for many months, and Hillary's State Department did nothing to improve security. Ambassador Stevens even made repeated requests for increased security, but to no avail.[270]

Just as important as it is to acknowledge Hillary's failure to provide proper security, it is critical to understand the geopolitical climate in Libya prior to the terrorist attack. The CIA was smuggling weapons out of Libya and sending them to Syria while they plotted to remove Gaddafi from power.[271] Hillary's emails would later point to these goals of the CIA and State Department.[272] It is suspected that both Hillary and the Obama administration were desperate to keep the truth of Benghazi secret, that was the reason for deleting her emails, and the reason that the Obama administration turned a blind eye to her criminal acts regarding her emails.[273]

Hillary's email scandal took center stage in the public arena during the 2016 U.S. Presidential Elections, and as of today, it is still a heated debate among both political parties, with no clear outcome as of yet.

What we do know, however, is that Hillary did indeed use a privately-owned email server physically located in her New York home to provide the web-hosting for a number of email accounts that she used both in her personal and professional life. This was in lieu of an @state.gov email account setup and hosted by the U.S. State Department following more stringent security protocols. Email addresses were hosted on her private server for at least the following domains:

@clintonemail.com, @wjcoffice.com, and @presidentclinton.com

Hillary contends that it "was just easier" to use a private email server and a single handheld BlackBerry device to address all of her email needs[274] and never used the @state.gov email.[275] Republican lawmakers and conservative news outlets are firm in their belief that Hillary conspired to have her emails hosted by her staff, so that she could bypass record-keeping laws.

Both Hillary and her staff were advised multiple times of the insecurity of her emails,[276] and it was suggested that they use an approved @state.gov or similar secure email, a suggestion she ignored on numerous occasions.[277]

For what it's worth, here is the one instance where I partially believe Hillary, well at least in part. I do not think that the *original intention* was to bypass federal record-keeping laws; that was merely a side benefit most likely not known until the Benghazi investigation. I believe premeditation on her part, in this case, would be giving far too much credit to Hillary and her staffers. It is far more likely that they wanted to keep the email process simple for Hillary, a non-tech-savvy individual.[278] Notwithstanding, I do feel that after it was made clear to Hillary on multiple occasions of the legal and security ramifications[279] of her private email server and BlackBerry usage, her refusal to comply does display a willingness to break the law and a total disregard for the security of classified information. She clearly felt as though she was above the law and could do as she pleased with impunity.

Very few took notice or care of the private email server until Hillary's emails were subpoenaed by Congress as part of their Benghazi investigation. On December 5, 2014, legal counsel for Clinton answered the subpoena and delivered 12 file boxes filled with printed paper containing more than 30,000 emails. However, a reported 32,000 emails were deleted and never provided to Congress. Through her lawyer, Hillary stated that "*[she] withheld almost 32,000 emails [her staff] deemed to be of a personal nature.*"[280] Her staff did not have proper security clearance to read and determine the 'personal nature' of said emails, and this avenue went without investigation by the FBI.

This is where the situation becomes a little bit more complicated. Through their investigation, Congress had requested emails from other persons involved in Benghazi as well, and they found emails to/from Hillary provided by these other persons in the conversation. The problem was that these messages were not included in the emails provided by Hillary's lawyers. Which means either out of carelessness or malice, she did not fully comply with the subpoena to produce all emails.

On March 4, 2015, Hillary was informed by Congress that she needs to keep all of her emails. This notice was accompanied by official subpoenas for all emails both work-related and personal.[281]

Less than three weeks later, Hillary blatantly defied the subpoena and instructed her staff to permanently delete all emails from the server in a manner that would all but guarantee they could never be recovered. Her computer techs used a software program called BleachBit to accomplish this.[282]

By March 27, 2015, Republican Congressman Trey Gowdy, Chairman of the Select Committee on Benghazi had enough of the deception and stated publicly that *"[Clinton] unilaterally decided to wipe her server clean"* and *"summarily decided to delete all emails."*[283] Clinton's attorney, David E. Kendall, said after an examination, no copies of any of Clinton's emails remained on the server. Kendall said the server was reconfigured only to retain emails for 60 days after Clinton's lawyers had decided which emails needed to be turned over. [284] This unilateral determination of a 60-day timeline is a direct violation of federal records keeping laws. And yet once again, Hillary is free to make up her own rules as she sees fit.

On June 22, 2015, after being deposed by the Benghazi committee, emails were publicly released between Clinton and longtime aide to the Clintons, Sidney Blumenthal. Many of these emails were never sent in by Clinton. In response to this blatant attempt from Hillary to subvert the requirements of law, Committee Chairman Gowdy issued a press release criticizing

Clinton for not providing the emails to the State Department.[285] Clinton originally said that she had provided all work-related emails to the State Department, and that only emails of a personal nature on her private server were destroyed. Her statement cannot be independently verified due to the email server being securely wiped of all data in a manner that would prevent any possible recovery of the missing emails. The act of deleting the emails is also a violation of federal law regarding the purposeful destruction of subpoenaed evidence.

The usage of a private email server located within her personal residence also brings up another possible violation of federal law. By taking classified documents out of a secure environment, such as the securely hosted @state.gov email servers, and placing it in her home server, she also committed the crime of theft by conversion. By converting government-owned documents and placing them for her own use in her house without prior permission, even if she was legally allowed to view or possess such documents, Hillary violated federal law. In fact, the law is very clear on this:

> *"Whoever embezzles, steals, purloins, or knowingly converts to his use or the use of another, or without authority, sells, conveys or disposes of any record, voucher, money, or thing of value of the United States or of any department or agency thereof, or any property made or being made under contract for the United States or any department or agency thereof; or . . . Whoever receives, conceals, or retains the same with intent to convert it to his use or gain, knowing it to have been embezzled, stolen, purloined or converted . . . Shall be fined under this title or imprisoned not*

more than ten years, or both; but if the value of such property in the aggregate, combining amounts from all the counts for which the defendant is convicted in a single case, does not exceed the sum of $1,000, he shall be fined under this title or imprisoned not more than one year, or both."[286]

To note, this crime would be imposed on a situational basis with each email converted for personal use considered a separate crime. This does not even touch the gross failure to maintain the security of classified information, nor the destruction of evidence under subpoena, nor her providing false statements to Congress, etc., etc., etc., all of which could send Hillary to prison for a very long time.

Yet all of these violations of federal law were ignored by the U.S. Justice Department because, at the time, it was believed by many that Hillary would win the 2016 election and nobody wanted to make an enemy of their presumed soon-to-be Commander in Chief. This includes U.S. Attorney General and longtime friend of the Clintons, Loretta Lynch; with her direct meddling in the investigation by telling the FBI not to call the email probe an "investigation,"[287] as to reduce any negative implications of guilt upon Hillary.[288]

"The establishment of the private server and its use with classified information plaintiff violated the law, all of here exists notwithstanding. And to those executes, the withholding, wiping and destruction of such huge amounts of email evidence removes all doubts about the intent and knowledge.", Doug Burns, U.S. Attorney Eastern District of New York[289]

On July 5, 2016, FBI Director James Comey, announced that no criminal charges would be sought against Hillary regarding her purposeful mishandling of classified emails. This announcement took many in the law enforcement community by surprise, including former Assistant FBI Director Steve Pomerantz:

"I could have fallen off my chair while watching the news conference. Setting aside the conclusion he drew, it was not the FBI's job to recommend prosecutions. The FBI investigates and then turns it over to the Department of Justice. In all my years in the FBI – over thirty years – and hundreds of investigations, probably thousands, I never ever saw that done. For Comey to do that was astonishing and wrong."[290]

Former federal prosecutor Doug Burns had a similar distaste for Comey's actions:

"It was beyond embarrassing to see the director of the FBI twist himself into a pretzel trying to explain the non-prosecution decision [of Clinton]... he violated every rule in the book; agents do not make prosecutorial decisions"[291]

Yet that is exactly what was done. Comey's FBI knew Hillary was guilty, yet they unilaterally decided to announce to the public that she was not criminally guilty. Yes, a prosecutor could have taken up the case. However, seeking a guilty verdict would be difficult after the head of the FBI went on national television saying she was not guilty.

Emails released in August of 2017 under FOIA requests from Judicial Watch, showed donors to the Clinton Foundation were getting special perks from the State Department while Hillary served as the Secretary of State.[292] Several emails showed *"the free flow of information and requests for favors between Clinton's State Department and the Clinton Foundation and major Clinton donors."*[293]

Once again, the Clintons got away with their crimes.

Russian Collusion

The Deep State, as of the time of this book, is beating the war drum about "Russian Collusion," referring to the completely disproven rumors that then-candidate Trump and now President Trump colluded with the Russian government to ensure his election win in 2016. The truth in the matter as the New York Times so eloquently put in their headline *"Cash Flowed to Clinton Foundation Amid Russian Uranium Deal,"*[294] the real collusion with Russia was with Bill and Hillary Clinton, and the Clinton Foundation was caught red-handed accepting millions of dollars from Russian interests during the Uranium One purchase.[295]

It was known by the U.S. government, as it is confirmed to have been reported to them on multiple occasions and by multiple informants, that the Russian government was paying bribes to guarantee the successful acquisition of Uranium One.

Theft of 2016 Election from Bernie

I am probably one of the last people you would catch with an *I'm With Bernie T-Shirt* on. He is a socialist that either has zero clue how basic economics works, or thinks the voting populace is too ignorant to realize everything he promised during his campaign would be financially impossible. Notwithstanding, our ideological differences in governance, the election was unjustly stolen from him by Hillary and the Democratic National Committee (DNC). In hindsight, Bernie should have been the Democratic candidate for the 2016 election instead of Hillary.

To explain how this happened to Bernie, let us take a look at the DNC and their poor financial health. After the 2012 Obama Campaign, the DNC was more than $24 million in debt with $15 million of that owed to banks and more than $8 million owed to various vendors.[296] This left the DNC in a financial quagmire that was almost impossible for them to extract themselves from without outside help. This is where the Hillary for America campaign and the Hillary Victory Fund (the joint fundraising apparatus with the DNC) paid off around $10 million worth of the DNC's debt in 2016 and placed the DNC on a monthly stipend to pay their overhead expenses. With this single stroke, the DNC handed over control away from DNC headquarters, to the Hillary camp in Brooklyn.

With this arrangement, Hillary was able to bypass the Federal Exchange Commission (FEC) law on campaign finance regulations that set a maximum donation by a single person to a presidential campaign at $2,700.[297] Now, a donor could 'legally' donate $353,400 to the Hillary Victory Fund, broken down as $10,000 to each of 32 states' parties, and $33,400 directly to the DNC. For battleground states, most of the money would stay at the state level to pay for various campaign-related expenses for the democratic nominee and the rest would be funneled to the DNC directly, and then immediately transferred to Hillary in Brooklyn. The amount kept by the states was less than one percent of the $82 million raised, the rest went to Hillary's campaign.[298]

An important item to note, was that this was taking place before Hillary was officially the nominee, and technically none of the funds should have been used to support a specific candidate. This was also during the time when Bernie was neck and neck with Hillary, and arguably had a leg up over the Republicans.

Then came the leaked emails, which revealed that the Hillary campaign was siphoning money from the individual state's democratic committees and using it to finance her campaign directly, not that of the party.

The Joint Fund-Raising Agreement between the DNC, the Hillary Victory Fund, and Hillary for America reads as follows:

> *"The agreement—signed by Amy Dacey, the former CEO of the DNC, and Robby Mook with a copy to Marc Elias—specified that in exchange for raising money and investing in the DNC, Hillary would control the party's finances, strategy, and all the money raised. Her campaign had the right of refusal of who would be the party communications director, and it would make final decisions on all the other staff. The DNC also was required to consult with the campaign about all other staffing, budgeting, data, analytics, and mailings."* [299]

This arrangement, while most likely not criminal, is indeed quite unethical to say the least. The ability for the Hillary camp to control staff hiring decisions, marketing, and expenditures of the DNC before she was voted as the nominee gave an unfair advantage to her. The game was most definitely rigged in her favor, even Senator Elizabeth Warren agreed when asked by CNN if *"Mrs. Clinton's contest against Democratic rival Bernie Sanders was rigged, and she said: 'Yes.'"*[300]

This was the one instance where even with her significant political power and the full support of the mainstream media, Hillary was simply an unlikable candidate, and was unable to win the presidential election.

BARACK OBAMA: THE WORST PRESIDENT IN US HISTORY

The people were so sick and tired of the neoconservatism brought on by the Bush & Cheney administration, they voted towards a new progressive leader in Barack Obama who promised change. What the American people got instead was the realization that the neo-cons were not limited to the Republican party. In fact, all we did was trade one oppressor for another; quite literally, a wolf in sheep's clothing.

Obama[DOESN'T]Care Act

The Affordable Care Act, or more commonly known as ObamaCare turned out to be one of the biggest shames in recent American history. A shame that was never questioned by the left-leaning media, as they did the bidding for the administration. It was the lies about this act that single-handedly gave Obama his second term in the White House.

When he introduced his plans, he assured the American people that under his leadership, the entire negotiation process would be open and clear to the public and broadcast on C-SPAN. Instead, it was another backroom-negotiated deal typical of the Deep State swamp without any public oversight. Obama's Press Secretary Robert Gibbs stated that *"[Obama] was in full agreement and wanted to get a bill to his desk as quickly as possible."*[301]

Not only did the public not know what was in the proposed act, most of Congress had no clue either. Nancy Pelosi remarked, *"we have to pass the bill, so that you can find out what's in it."* Obviously, his promise for transparency and bipartisanship was to be tossed out the window. All that mattered was getting the act passed.

If that was the only issue with the ACA, then one could *almost* overlook the lack of transparency if it helped reduce political posturing and grandstanding in the public eye, and accomplished the mission of providing *Affordable* healthcare to all.

When selling it to the public, Obama claimed that *"if you like your health care plan, you can keep it."* This turned out to be a complete lie.[302] This lie was so big, that it even earned Obama the *2013 Lie of the Year* award from PolitiFact[303] after millions of Americans began to receive cancellation notices from their insurance companies, informing them their current plans were not ACA-compliant and were no longer available.

There was also the claim that consumers would find a savings of upwards of $2,500 per person; this was known to be a complete distortion of the facts. *"Premiums for individual coverage more than doubled between 2013 and 2017."* [304] These were facts known by senior officials, including Obama, that the *"numbers just did not add up."*

On top of that, is the over $319 million dollars[305] spent on building the horrible HealthCare.gov online marketplace, a system that failed so miserably on its initial launch, it was only able to successfully enroll a total of six people on the first day.[306] Obama was informed prior to the launch of the website that it was incapable of handling the projected amount of web traffic and had serious privacy and security-related concerns.[307] The privacy and security concerns of millions of Americans turned out to be of no concern for Obama because he wanted the system launched.[308]

Muammar Gaddafi

Under his reign, the people of Libya lived with a higher standard of living than most of Africa, and he had the support of most of his people, but of course, he did have some very powerful enemies. In 2010, some of these enemies began to protest him. Protests soon turned into insurrection led by Islamic extremists, including Al Qaeda's North African affiliate.[309]

Gaddafi was able to squash most of the resistance quickly, with the exception of Benghazi, a stronghold of al-Qaeda at the time. The neo-cons in the Obama administration were hellbent on defeating Gaddafi and began spreading rumors that Gaddafi *"pledged to create a bloodbath in Benghazi."*[310] Based upon these rumors, the neo-cons wrote a letter and had it signed by 40 members of the Foreign Policy Initiative to pressure the Obama administration into using military action to topple Gaddafi.[311]

The *Washington Post* wrote in support of this course of action, *"the [Washington] Post's editors demanded that Obama take the lead in implementing a military strategy that ensures regime change in Tripoli."*[312]

Our old friend Hillary was Secretary of State at the time and supported wholeheartedly the policy of removing Gaddafi. In fact, she was so strong in her support that she served as the driving force in pressuring Obama to take action; it was commonly referred to as "Hillary's War."[313]   Under her direction, the U.S. was left more vulnerable to terrorist attacks.[314] Months later, she would be quoted on CBS as saying "We came, we saw, he died!"[315]

Once again, we were in a military battle with a foreign power based upon lies to the American people. An estimated 233 deaths took place in Benghazi, far less than the supposed bloodbath of tens of thousands that was being portrayed, and out of those 233, most were al-Qaeda terrorists.[316] So, why did we help al-Qaeda in their fight against Gaddafi?

The U.S. had two strategic goals that required Gaddafi to be removed from power.[317] With him out of the way, the CIA could transfer Libya's weapons cache to anti-Assad rebels in Syria.[318] The second reason, was that Gaddafi was threatening to create his own African-based currency that would be used to purchase Libyan oil. This would threaten the U.S. Dollar as the standard petrol dollar,[319] and in fact, was the very same mistake that Saddam made.

Gaddafi was identified, tracked down, and killed. With success in the air, Mrs. Clinton took a tour of the country and proclaimed Libya liberated.[320]   Of course, just as history would predict, the county turned out no better than past instances of regime change by the neo-cons. Within months, the country was in chaos. This chaos would eventually lead to the 2012 attacks against the U.S. Consulate in Benghazi.

Years later, then Secretary of Defense Leon Panetta would admit that the entire reason for going to Libya was never humanitarian as claimed in the media, *our goal in Libya was regime change.*"[321]

In 2016, the U.K. Parliament report on Libya said that it was based, like the Iraq war, on lies.[322]

On March 4, 2017, President Donald J. Trump tweeted, *"Terrible! Just found out that Obama had my 'wires tapped' in Trump Tower just before the victory. Nothing found. This is McCarthyism!"*[323] This was then followed up a few follow-up tweets:

Donald J. Trump ✓
@realDonaldTrump

Terrible! Just found out that Obama had my "wires tapped" in Trump Tower just before the victory. Nothing found. This is McCarthyism!

♡ 140K   6:35 AM - Mar 4, 2017

♡ 101K people are talking about this

Donald J. Trump ✓
@realDonaldTrump

Is it legal for a sitting President to be "wire tapping" a race for president prior to an election? Turned down by court earlier. A NEW LOW!

♡ 123K   6:49 AM - Mar 4, 2017

♡ 71.4K people are talking about this

Donald J. Trump ✓
@realDonaldTrump

I'd bet a good lawyer could make a great case out of the fact that President Obama was tapping my phones in October, just prior to Election!

♡ 126K   6:52 AM - Mar 4, 2017

♡ 76.1K people are talking about this

Donald J. Trump ✓
@realDonaldTrump

How low has President Obama gone to tapp my phones during the very sacred election process. This is Nixon/Watergate. Bad (or sick) guy!

♡ 159K   7:02 AM - Mar 4, 2017

♡ 154K people are talking about this

The mere accusation of using the power of the White House to spy on a political opponent should have stirred the media into a feeding frenzy, with immediate demands for investigations of Obama, but of course, we all know better than that. The media would never turn on their love for Obama.

Obama spokesperson, Kevin Lewis, issued a statement the following day that read in part, "*A cardinal rule of the Obama administration was that no White House official ever interfered with any independent investigation led by the Department of Justice. As part of that practice, neither President Obama nor any White House official ever ordered surveillance on any U.S. citizen. Any suggestion otherwise is simply false.*"[324]

Of course, like so many other statements made by career politicians with law degrees, the statement was not exactly a denial of the subject at hand, nor was it factually incorrect. He stated he never ordered it, he did not say he did not know about it. There is a subtle distinction, yes, but it allowed Obama to skirt the issue and answer a different question while appearing to answer the original question.

A formal denial, of course, would have been impossible and illegal because there was a wiretap, and Obama knew it. Obama speechwriter, Jon Favreau, warned journalists not to report that there had been no wiretap at all.[325] "*I'd be careful about reporting that Obama said there was no wiretapping. [you should report] neither he nor the WH ordered it.*"[326]

The issue is, the media already knew about the wiretaps. In fact, months earlier on Trump's Inauguration Day, the front-page headline of the New York Times was titled "*Wiretapped Data Used in Inquiry of Trump Aides.*" Now with Trump calling Obama out on this, the *Times* quietly changed the online version of the article to say, "*Intercepted Russian Communications Part of Inquiry Intro Trump Associates,*"[327] to save face and protect Obama.

This data eventually resulted in the resignation of Trump's National Security Advisor, Michael Flynn,[328] due to the political optics of the situation when he lied to cover up a conversation he had with Russia, a conversation that was later proven to be fully legal.

However, it is still important to note that as of the time of writing this book, absolutely no evidence has been found to implicate Donald J. Trump in any illegal dealings with Russia.

The investigation began in the spring of 2016, when the White House and the Department of Justice pursued a criminal investigation of Trumps' associates, and perhaps Trump himself, over concerns of his alleged Russian connections.[329] As we all now know, the investigation found no crimes committed by Trump and rather than ending their investigation, they pivoted into a national-security investigation, allowing them to continuing spying on the campaign.

As a law and order man myself, I understand the need of our national law enforcement and intelligence agencies to investigate any suspected interference by foreign powers upon our elections. On the surface, it appeared as though this was what the FBI and NSA were doing. However, upon digging deeper, it became abundantly clear the goal was to destroy then-candidate Trump from winning the election. And then after he won, it turned into an investigation to destroy Trump's presidency. And when those two missions failed, it has now turned into an investigation to prevent Trump from winning re-election.

In April of 2017, CNN reported that the FBI used a thirty-five-page document to obtain the original FISA court approval for wiretapping the Trump Campaign as part of their investigation into possible Russian meddling in the 2016 election.[330] That document has come to be known as the *anti-Trump dossier* which was full of allegations against Donald Trump. The first problem is that this document was produced by a company named Fusion GPS as opposition research by the Clinton Campaign, where they hired former British spy, Christopher Steele, to investigate connections between Trump and Russia.[331]

In and of itself, this doesn't discredit any possible facts contained within the dossier. It is completely reasonable to presume it would be incumbent upon the Clinton campaign to turn over any evidence they *stumbled upon* that could implicate Russian meddling. However, that was not how this took place. Instead of being forthcoming with their suspicions, the campaign continued to finance the '*research*' into Trump and they used the FBI as their personal Gestapo.

State Judiciary Committee Chairman Chuck Grassley was less than pleased when he learned of this and was quoted as saying, "*The idea that the FBI and associates of the Clinton campaign would pay Mr. Steele to investigate the Republican nominee for President in the run-up to the election raise further questions about the FBI's independence from politics, as well as the Obama administration's use of law enforcement and intelligence agencies for political ends.*" [332]

Even FBI Director James Comey had his doubts on the legitimacy of the information contained in the dossier when he described it as being full of *"salacious and unverified"* material in his testimony before the Senate Select Committee on Intelligence.[333]

Once again playing the devil's advocate here, it is incumbent upon law enforcement to investigate all claims of crimes, even if the claim appears on the outside to be less than optimal. However, my objection is in how they lied to the FISA court. As part of the application process, they must testify that the evidence they present to the court is accurate to the best of their knowledge. Comey has already said that he did not have high confidence in the reliability of the information, yet, he approved the investigation to continue.

Furthermore, the FBI should have informed the court of the source of the dossier data. They hid that information because they knew it would force the court to be more skeptical and they may not have taken it at face value.

Evidence that the FBI did not have any strong evidence without the use of the dossier lies in the fact that the FISA court originally turned down the request for a warrant; which is something that almost never happens.[334] It was only after the dossier was brought to the court that they finally received the approval.

Just as troubling, we know that Steele was in repeated contact with an associate Deputy Attorney General in the Obama Justice Department.[335] This brings up serious concerns as to just how involved Obama was and if this was a trap being set to catch Trump.

Part III:

The American People Caught in the Middle

THE ELECTION OF
DONALD J. TRUMP

The neo-cons/powerful elites or the Deep State, as we refer to them, were so entrenched in the status quo that they are all suffering a group delusion. Members of the media have coined the phrase *Trump Derangement Syndrome* to refer to those that suffer from this psychosis. These political and social elites are completely flabbergasted and in denial of the presidential election. In their minds, democracy has failed, as there is no other reasonable explanation, at least to their logic, for Trump to have won the election.

Within days of the Trump presidency, Democratic Congresswoman Maxine Waters was already beating the war drum for impeachment.[336]

During the 2016 election, radical hate groups self-identifying themselves as Antifa found support from the far left in their battle against Trump. These supposed anti-fascist groups, in fact, were anything but ANTI-fascist in their ideologies or public displays. Hitler describes in his book *Mein Kampf* how "*his brownshirts would come to political events, typically held in bars and beer halls, armed with bats and sticks.*"[337] Ironically for an organization that claims to fight fascism, it is they who actually follow fascist dogma by using the same tactics that worked perfectly for Hitler.

Antifa members dress up in all black, with masks covering their faces, sticks, and other weapons. At political protests, Antifa physically demonstrates their opposition with violence against any dissenting opinion, in this case, support for Trump.

Today, we find ourselves at a point in time where those in power are so desperate to remain in power, they will do anything to maintain the status quo. Political parties of Republicans or Democrats, and political ideologies alike have been hijacked to divide and conquer the populous and keep the people ignorant as to whom is really pulling the strings.

The surprising turn of events was the 2016 election when the Republican party turned away from their historical support for the big business of Wall Street and focused on the working class. Was this altruistic or just pure dumb luck, who knows? Either way, the party started fighting for the forgotten folks in middle America.

The truth is that the real fascists have infiltrated the left and brand themselves under the more socially acceptable term of democratic socialism. The party is split into multiple competing factions, each trying to outdo the other with even grander social entitlements. They only thing they can collectively agree upon is their hatred for Trump and to heavily tax the wealthy to provide the poor with everything for free.

Economist Friedrich Hayek surmised it so eloquently in his 1944 book *The Road to Serfdom,* that the Western entitlements supported by the left were moving inexorably into the direction of fascism. *"The rise of fascism and Nazism was not a reaction against the socialist trends of the preceding period but a necessary outcome of those tendencies."*[338]

MAINSTREAM MEDIA BIAS "FAKE NEWS"

The question is how are the Antifa getting their misinformation and misdirected hatred towards Trump? In a simple phrase that the Donald likes to use himself "Fake News". As Joseph Goebbels, the Nazi Minister of Propaganda said, *"Propaganda is always a means to an end. The propaganda that produces the desired result is good and all other propaganda is bad."*[339]

> *"[The U.S. mainstream media] are effective and powerful ideological institutions that carry out a system-supportive propaganda function, by reliance on market forces, internalized assumptions, and self-censorship, and without overt coercion"*[340]

Columnist Richard Cohen of the Washington Post suggested the country's need for a constitutional coup, where the elected officials remove the President because they feel he is *"unable to discharge the powers and duties of his office."*[341] This lunacy isn't limited to one reporter or one publication. James Kirchick for the Los Angeles Times stated, *"Trump is not only patently unfit to be President, but a danger to America and the world. Voters must stop him before the military has to."*[342]

The media has been on the side of the Deep State and has adamantly fought against the truth coming out to the people.

Case in point, the media attacking the 9/11 Truth Movement and demanding investigations into the members of the truth movement, while simultaneously ignoring the claims of a coverup by high ranking government officials. [343]

Putting aside the obviousness of political hypocrisy of the talking heads at CNN, MSNBC, and other left-leaning news outlets; a larger concern is big tech.

Conclusions

My choice to write about the wrongs of both the 'right' and the 'left' was probably not a wise decision, if my goal was strictly to sell books. If I would have chosen either one side or the other, I could be assured of countless supporters eager to hear the dirt "on the other guy." America is very tribal in nature. Very few people actually take the time to step back and look at the whole picture.

Bill Clinton, aside from his abhorrent acts of sexual misconduct by raping countless women, was a decent President. He, like all humans, made some bad decisions during his presidency and made some good decisions. He was and probably still is addicted to sex and there have been plenty of women willing to have sex with him because of who he is. Regarding the actions of cheating on his wife, this is the personal business of his family and not that of the world. If he could have kept his actions limited to consensual sexual encounters and not also rape women against their will, history would have been much kinder to him. He will rightfully go down in the history books as one of the worst individuals, on a personal level, to ever sit in the Oval Office.

Most politicians are not *pure evil,* as the other side likes to portray them. Each of them will do what it takes to get in power and stay in power, and as long as we continue to vote in the same group of people from the swamp, nothing will change. Their goal is absolute power and their modus operandi is simple: divide and conquer.

The Democratic party operates on the same old playbook that the Republicans are racist, homophobic, xenophobic, misogynistic, and Islamophobic. These fears get the base of predominantly white, apologetic, college students from wealthy families all touting the talking points to be used as weapons against the Republicans. Then, conversely, the Republican party beats the same war-drums of national-security; sending our troops to fight battles that have little to do with actually securing our country and more to do with making money for rich oil and military contractors.

I feel that this is why the country went against the swamp and voted President Trump into office. Is he perfect? Hell no; he has many flaws. However, he takes a personal joy out of pissing off the swamp when he calls them out for their corruption. He is making decisions on public policy with the intent of improving the outcome for America. He has made some stumbles along the way due to his ignorance of political decorum, but wasn't that what we, the people, liked about him when we voted? We wanted the swamp drained.

Will Trump remove all of the corruption out of politics? No, because it is against human nature and I am fine with that, just as long as the country is left better than when he found it. With this understanding of life in mind, I do not care that the Clintons profited from their positions in public office because all politicians have in the past, currently do now, and will do so in the future. The issue is when they, our elected representatives, use their power to cover up crimes and purposefully make decisions that impact the lives of Americans, not for the betterment of the country, but for the profit or political gains of the few.

Endnotes

1   Moïse, Edwin E. (1996). Tonkin Gulf and the Escalation of the Vietnam War. Chapel Hill: University of North Carolina Press. ISBN 0-8078-2300-7.

2   Robert J. Hanyok, "Skunks, Bogies, Silent Hounds, and the Flying Fish: The Gulf of Tonkin Mystery, 2–4 August 1964" Cryptologic Quarterly, Winter 2000/Spring 2001 Edition, Vol. 19, No. 4 / Vol. 20, No. 1. (https://web.archive.org/web/20160131235457/http://www.nsa.gov/public_info/_files/gulf_of_tonkin/articles/rel1_skunks_bogies.pdf)

3   Moïse, Edwin E. (1996). Tonkin Gulf and the Escalation of the Vietnam War. Chapel Hill: University of North Carolina Press. ISBN 0-8078-2300-7.

4   Wise, David (1973). The Politics of Lying: government deception, secrecy, and power. New York: Vintage Books. ISBN 0-394-47932-7.

5   Moïse, Edwin E. (1996). Tonkin Gulf and the Escalation of the Vietnam War. Chapel Hill: University of North Carolina Press. ISBN 0-8078-2300-7.

6   Robert Parry. "Consortiumnews.com". (http://www.consortiumnews.com/2008/011108a.html)

7   U.S.G ed., IV.C.1, pp. 1-3; Gravel ed., III:17-18.

8   President Johnson and Robert Anderson, 9:46 AM, Aug, 3 1964, Tape WH6408.03, Citation #4632, LBJ Recordings

9   Bamford, James in Body of Secrets, Anchor, Reprint edition (April 30, 2002), ISBN 978-0385499088

10   Robert J. Hanyok, "Skunks, Bogies, Silent Hounds, and the Flying Fish: The Gulf of Tonkin Mystery, 2–4 August 1964" Cryptologic Quarterly, Winter 2000/Spring 2001 Edition, Vol. 19, No. 4 / Vol. 20, No. 1. (https://web.archive.org/web/20160131235457/http://www.nsa.gov/public_info/_files/gulf_of_tonkin/articles/rel1_skunks_bogies.pdf)

11   The Fog of War, Documentary, 2003 (https://www..amazon.com/
Fog-War-Robert-McNamara/dp/B0001L3LUE/ref=sr_1_2?ie=UTF8&-
qid=1530217881&sr=8-2)

12   Kornbluh, Peter & Byrne, Malcolm The Iran-Contra Scandal: A Declassified
History, New York: New Press, 1993 page 213.

13   Stork, Joe; Lesch, Ann M. "Background to the Crisis: Why War?". Middle
East Report. Middle East Research and Information Project (MERIP) (167,
November–December 1990): 11–18. JSTOR 3012998. (https://www.jstor.org/
stable/3012998 -- subscription required)

14   Blight, James G.; et al. (2012). Becoming Enemies: U.S.-Iran Relations and
the Iran-Iraq War, 1979-1988. Rowman & Littlefield Publishers. pp. 20–21,
97,

15   Yaphe, Judith (2013). "Changing American Perspectives on the Iran-Iraq
war". The Iran-Iraq War: New International Perspectives. Routledge. ISBN
9780415685245.

16   Friedman, Alan. Spider's Web: The Secret History of How the White House
Illegally Armed Iraq, Bantam Books, 1993.

17   Harris, Shane; Aid, Matthew M. (2013-08-26). "Exclusive: CIA Files Prove
America Helped Saddam as He Gassed Iran". Foreign Policy. Retrieved 2017-
05-07.

18   The American-Israeli Cooperative Enterprise. Retrieved 7 June 2008. (https://
www.jewishvirtuallibrary.org/jsource/U.S.-Israel/Iran_Contra_Affair.html)

19   Kornbluh, Peter & Byrne, Malcolm The Iran-Contra Scandal: A Declassified
History, New York: New Press, 1993 page 214.

20   Reagan, Ronald (1990), p. 504

21   Kornbluh, Peter & Byrne, Malcolm The Iran-Contra Scandal: A Declassified
History, New York: New Press, 1993 page 214.

22   Kornbluh, Peter & Byrne, Malcolm The Iran-Contra Scandal: A Declassified
History, New York: New Press, 1993 page 214.

23   United States. Congress. House. Select Committee to Investigate Covert Arms
Transactions with Iran; United States. Congress. Senate. Select Committee
on Secret Military Assistance to Iran and the Nicaraguan Opposition (8 May
1987). "Report of the congressional committees investigating the Iran- Contra
Affair : with supplemental, minority, and additional views". Washington : U.S.

House of Representatives Select Committee to Investigate Covert Arms Transactions with Iran : U.S. Senate Select Committee on Secret Military Assistance to Iran and the Nicaraguan Opposition : For sale by the Supt. of Docs., U.S. G.P.O. – via Internet Archive.
(https://archive.org/details/reportofcongress87unit)

24   "Excerpts from the Tower Commission's Report", January 26, 1987.
(http://www.presidency.ucsb.edu/PS157/assignment%20files%20public/
TOWER%20EXCERPTS.htm#PartII)

25   Kornbluh, Peter & Byrne, Malcolm The Iran-Contra Scandal: A Declassified History, New York: New Press, 1993 page 250

26   Koppel, Ted. The U.S.S Vincennes: Public War, Secret War, ABC Nightline. July 1, 1992. (https://web.archive.org/web/20040824084457/http://home-page.ntlworld.com/jksonc/docs/ir655-nightline-19920701.html)

27   Cave, George. "Why Secret 1986 U.S.-Iran 'Arms for Hostages' Negotiations Failed". Washington Report on Middle Eastern Affairs. Retrieved 9 January 2007.
(http://www.wrmea.com/backissues/0994/9409008.htm)

28   Reagan, Ronald (November 13, 1986). "Address to the Nation on the Iran Arms and Contra Aid Controversy". Ronald Reagan Presidential Foundation. Retrieved 7 June 2008.
(http://www.reagan.utexas.edu/archives/speeches/1986/111386c.htm)

29   Subcommittee on Terrorism, Narcotics, and International Communications and International Economic Policy, Trade, Oceans, and Environment of the Committee on Foreign Relations, United States Senate (1989). Drugs, law enforcement, and foreign policy : A report. Washington: GPO. (https://babel.hathitrust.org/cgi/pt?id=pst.000014976124;view=1up;seq=3)

30   Greg Szymanski. "Former DEA Agent Wants George H. Bush, Negroponte and Other Higher-Ups Held Accountable for Illegal Drug Smuggling", March 5, 2006

31   Timothy Lange, Daily Kos, 27 December 2009, Blast from the Past. Gene Hasenfus: December 1986 (http://www.dailykos.com/sto-ry/2009/12/27/819675/-Blast-from-the-Past-Gene-Hasenfus-December-1986)

32   Walsh, Lawrence (August 4, 1993). "Vol. I: Investigations and prosecutions". Final report of the independent counsel for Iran/Contra matters. Independent Council for Iran/Contra Matters. Retrieved 15 May 2009.
(https://fas.org/irp/offdocs/walsh/)

33   http://www.nytimes Archived 11 July 2013 at the Wayback Machine., July 21, 1988, "Civil Liberties Union Asks Court to Quash Iran-Conta Indictment" by Philip Shannon (https://web.archive.org/web/20130711135055/http://nytimes/)

34   "The Iran-Contra Affair 20 Years On". Gwu.edu. Retrieved 2014-08-18. (http://www.gwu.edu/~nsarchiv/NSAEBB/NSAEBB210/index.htm)

35   "National Security Directive 26" (PDF). The White House. 1989-10-02. Retrieved 2006-10-12. (http://www.fas.org/irp/offdocs/nsd/nsd26.pdf)

36   In war, some facts less factual, Scott Peterson, The Christian Science Monitor, September 6, 2002 http://www.csmonitor.com/2002/0906/p01s02-wosc.html

37   Heller, Jean (1991-01-06). "Photos don't show buildup". St. Petersburg Times.

38   CSPAN Video Recording (https://www.youtube.com/watch?v=Lm-fVs3WaE9Y)

39   Krauss, Clifford (January 12, 1992). "Congressman Says Girl Was Credible". The New York Times. (https://www.nytimes.com/1992/01/12/world/congress-man-says-girl-was-credible.html)

40   Brosnan, James W. (October 11, 1990). "Witnesses describe atrocities by Iraqis". The Commercial Appeal.

41   http://www.dougwalton.ca/papers%20in%20pdf/95Pity.pdf

42   Arthur, John (January 6, 1992). "Remember Nayirah, Witness for Kuwait?". The New York Times.

43   Cohen, Mitchel (December 28, 2002). "How George Bush, Sr. Sold the 1991 Bombing of Iraq to America". CounterPunch. (https://web.archive.org/web/20110429012920/http://www.counterpunch.org/cohen1228.html)

44   http://www.counterpunch.org/cohen1228.html

45   Ted Rowse, "Kuwaitgate - killing of Kuwaiti babies by Iraqi soldiers exagger-ated," Washington Monthly (September 1992). (http://findarticles.com/p/articles/mi_m1316/is_n9_v24/ai_12529902/)

46   U.S. Senate Banking Committee. Second Staff Report on U.S. CBW-Related Dual-Use Exports to Iraq, May 25, 1994. (http://www.gulfwarvets.com/arison/banking.htm)

47   Riegle, Jr., Donald W. U.S. Chemical and Biological Warfare-Related Dual

Use Exports to Iraq and their Possible Impact on the Health Consequences of the Gulf War, Committee on Banking, Housing and Urban Affairs, May 25, 1994. (http://www.gulfweb.org/bigdoc/report/riegle1.html)

48   "Nine facts about terrorism in the United States since 9/11". The Washington Post. September 11, 2013. (https://www.washingtonpost.com/news/wonk/wp/2013/09/11/nine-facts-about-terrorism-in-the-united-states-since-911/)

49   "Suspect 'reveals 9/11 planning'". BBC News. September 22, 2003. (http://news.bbc.co.uk/2/hi/south_asia/3128802.stm)

50   Lichtblau, Eric (March 20, 2003). "Bin Laden Choose 9/11 Targets, al-Qaeda Leader Says". The New York Times. (https://query.nytimes.com/gst/fullpage.html?res=9404E7DF1031F933A15750C0A9659C8B63)

51   "National Commission on Terrorist Attacks Upon the United States". 9-11commission.gov. Retrieved 2011-09-11. (http://www.9-11commission.gov/report/911Report_Ch5.htm)

52   "Fact Sheet: Updated State Dept List of Identified Terrorists and Groups". Fas.org. Retrieved 2011-09-11.
(http://www.fas.org/irp/news/2002/10/dos101102.html)

53   Computerworld Magazine September 3, 2006 (https://web.archive.org/web/20060903074522/http://www.computerworld.com/securitytopics/security/story/0,10801,77682,00.html)

54   "Wahhabis in the Old Dominion". Theweeklystandard.com. 2002-04-08. R(http://www.theweeklystandard.com/Content/Public/Articles/000/000/001/072kqska.asp)

55   October 3, 2003, at the Wayback Machine. (https://web.archive.org/web/20031003130110/http://wbz4.com/iteam/local_story_343145212.html)

56   "Primetime Investigation FBI Terrorist Cover Up". Billstclair.com. 2002-12-19. Archived from the original on 2006-02-13. Retrieved 2011-09-1 (https://web.archive.org/web/20060213211232/http://billstclair.com/911timeline/2002/abcnews121902b.html)

57   Boston Globe, Frank Davies, September 5, 2004 (http://archive.boston.com/news/nation/articles/2004/09/05/911_hijackers_tied_to_saudi_government_graham_says_in_book/)

58   "National Commission on Terrorist Attacks Upon the United States". 9-11commission.gov. (http://www.9-11commission.gov/report/911Report_Ch5.htm)

59   Wright, Lawrence (2006), The Looming Tower: Al-Qaeda and the Road to 9/11, Knopf, ISBN 978-0-375-41486-2

60   Wright, Lawrence (2006), The Looming Tower: Al-Qaeda and the Road to 9/11, Knopf, ISBN 978-0-375-41486-2 pp. 310–312.

61   Wright, Lawrence (2006), The Looming Tower: Al-Qaeda and the Road to 9/11, Knopf, ISBN 978-0-375-41486-2 pp. 235–236

62   Wright, Lawrence (2006), The Looming Tower: Al-Qaeda and the Road to 9/11, Knopf, ISBN 978-0-375-41486-2 pp. 242–243

63   Lt. Col. Shaffer's Written Testimony: Able Danger and the 9/11 Attacks, Armed Services Committee, US House of Representatives, February 15, 2006

64   Lt. Col. Shaffer's Written Testimony: Able Danger and the 9/11 Attacks, Armed Services Committee, US House of Representatives, February 15, 2006

65   Kean-Hamilton Statement on Able Danger, August 12 2005

66   Senator Joe Biden's comment during September 21, 2005, Senate Hearing

67   David Ray Griffin and Elizabeth Woodworth, 9/11 Unmasked: An International Review Panel Investigation, p 186

68   Able Danger and Intelligence Information Sharing, Hearing before the Committee on the Judiciary, United States Senate, September 21, 2005. (https://www.gpo.gov/fdsys/pkg/CHRG-109shrg25409/html/CHRG-109shrg25409.htm)

69   "Greg Palest report transcript - 6/11/01". BBC News. November 8, 2001. Retrieved May 22, 2010. (http://news.bbc.co.uk/1/hi/events/newsnight/1645527.stm)

70   Wright, Lawrence (2006), The Looming Tower: Al-Qaeda and the Road to 9/11, Knopf, ISBN 978-0-375-41486-2 pp. 350

71   Snippet from the film The Spymasters: CIA in the Crosshairs

72   Chris Whipple, The Attacks Will be Spectacular, Politico, November 12, 2015

73   "THE OSAMA BIN LADEN FILE: National Security Archive Electronic Briefing Book No. 343". The National Security Archive. The National Security Archive. Retrieved March 14, 2016. (http://nsarchive.gwu.edu/NSAEBB/NSAEBB343/)

74   Wright, Lawrence (2006), The Looming Tower: Al-Qaeda and the Road to 9/11, Knopf, ISBN 978-0-375-41486-2 pp. 350 - 351

75   The 9/11 Commission Report: Final Report of the National Commission on Terrorist Attacks upon the United States, Authorized Edition (W.W. Norton, 2004), p 541

76   Lipton, Eric (August 22, 2008). "Fire, Not Explosives, Felled 3rd Tower on 9/11, Report Says". The New York Times. Archived from the original on March 9, 2011. (https://web.archive.org/web/20110309235941/http://www. nytimes.com/2008/08/22/nyregion/22wtccnd.html)

77   Roemer's statement made during 9/11 Commission hearing (http://www.9-11commission.gov/archive/hearing11/9-11Commission_Hearing_2004-05-18.htm)

78   Oral History: Father John Delendick (https://graphics8.nytimes.com/packages/pdf/nyregion/20050812_WTC_GRAPHIC/9110230.PDF)

79   David Ray Griffin and Elizabeth Woodworth, 9/11 Unmasked: An International Review Panel Investigation, p157

80   Beam, Christopher (April 8, 2009). "Heated Controversy". Slate. (https://web.archive.org/web/20090518074848/http://www.slate.com/id/2215703)

81   Architects & Engineers for 9/11 Truth (June 30, 2009). "Architect to Speak in D.C. on 9/11 World Trade Center Destruction". PRNewswire-U.S.Newswire. (http://news.prnewswire.com/DisplayReleaseContent.aspx?ACCT=104&STORY=/www/story/06-30-2009/0005053117)

82   Potocki, P. Joseph (August 27, 2008). "Down the 9-11 Rabbit Hole". Bohemian. (https://web.archive.org/web/20090604091229/http://www.bohemian.com/bohemian/08.27.08/cover-911.truth-0835.html)

83   Beam, Alex (Jan 14, 2008). "The truth is out there . . . Isn't it?". The Boston Globe. (https://web.archive.org/web/20090603232630/http://www.boston.com/ae/tv/articles/2008/01/14/the_truth_is_out_there____isnt_it)

84   Lachapelle, Judith (May 1, 2010). "Le "mystère" de la Tour 7". La Presse. (https://web.archive.org/web/20100503003859/http://www.cyberpresse.ca/international/en-vedette/201005/01/01-4276172-le-mystere-de-la-tour-7.php)

85   "Un arquitecto estadounidense presenta en Madrid su versión alternativa al 11-S". Telecinco. November 8, 2008. El ingeniero estructural del complejo WTC, advierte Gage, llama la atención sobre la piscina de magma que ardió durante semanas tras el atentado. Una evidencia que demuestra la existencia del

agente incendiario 'Thermite', empleado para "fundir y cortar columnas y vigas de acero. (http://www.telecinco.es/informativos/internacional/noticia/51928/ Un+arquitecto+estadounidense+presenta+su+version+alternativa+al+11S+en+- Madrid)

86   Steven Jones, Robert Korol, Anthony Szamboti, and Ted Walter, 15 Years Later: On the Physics of High-rise Building Collapses, Europhysics News, July-August 2016: 22-26

87   "Questions and Answers about the NIST WTC 7 Investigation". NIST. (https://www.nist.gov/public_affairs/factsheet/wtc_qa_082108.cfm)

88   "Questions and Answers about the NIST WTC 7 Investigation". NIST. (https://www.nist.gov/public_affairs/factsheet/wtc_qa_082108.cfm)

89   Gage, Richard; Roberts, Gregg; Chandler, David. "Conspiracy theory or hidden truth? The 9/11 enigmas." World Architecture News. (http://www.worldarchitecturenews.com/index.php?fuseaction=wanappln.commentview&comment_id=158)

90   Beam, Christopher (April 8, 2009). "Heated Controversy". Slate. (https://web.archive.org/web/20090518074848/http://www.slate.com/id/2215703)

91   A Nation Challenged: The Site, Engineers Half a Culprit in the Strange Collapse of 7 World Trade Center: Diesel Fuel, New York Times, November 29, 2001.

92   NIST, Answers to Frequently Asked Questions, August 30, 2006, Question #2

93   Graeme MacQueen, 118 Witnesses: The Firefighters' Testimony to Explosions in the Twin Towers, the Journal of 9/11 Studies, Vol 2, August 2006, pg 47-106.

94   David Ray Griffin, Explosive Testimony: Revelations about the Twin Towers in the 9/11 Oral Histories, 911Truth.org, January 18, 2006.

95   NIST NCSTAR 1, Final Report on the Collapse of the World Trade Center Towers, September 2005: xxxviii

96   Federal Emergency Management Agency (2002), World Trade Center Building Performance Study: Data Collection, Preliminary Observations, and Recommendations.

97   Twin Tower Fires Not Hot Enough to Melt or Weaken Steel!, YouTube: 9/11 Truth Videos.

98   FEMA, World Trade Center Building Performance Study, Chapter 5, Section 6.2, "Probable Collapse Sequence".

99   NIST NCSTAR 1A, Final Report on the Collapse of World Trade Center Building 7, November 2008

100 The 9/11 Commission Report, p 302

101 Federal Bureau of Investigations, Most Wanted Terrorists, (http://web.archive.org/web/2010101161759/http://www.fbi.gov/wanted/topten/usama-bin-laden)

102 Ed Haas, FBI says: ' No Hard Evidence Connecting Bin Laden to 9/11', (http://web.archive.org/web/20090207113442/www.teamliberty.net/id267.html)

103 Curtis Taylor, Newsday, September 12, 2001 (http://web.archive.org/web/20050127000302/http:/www.nynewsday.com/news/local/manhattan/wtc/ny-nyaler122362178sep12,0,6794009.story)

104 Diplomat, Luke Hunt, The. "Former Warlord Primed For Afghan Presidency". The Diplomat.

105 "Operation Enduring Freedom Fast Facts". CNN. (http://www.cnn.com/2013/10/28/world/operation-enduring-freedom-fast-facts/index.html)

106 Gary Webb & Pamela Kramer, Series on CIA-Run Drug Rings Sparks Call for Probe, San Jose Mercury News, August 29, 1996, p. 1

107 CNN, U.S. Afghan Poppy Production Doubles, November 29, 2003, p 1.

108 President Bush Outlines Iraqi Threat". White House news release (Press release). The White House. 2002-10-07. (https://georgewbush-whitehouse.archives.gov/news/releases/2002/10/print/20021007-8.html)

109 Link between Saddam and al-Qaeda - ABC News video report (http://www.mediaresearch.org/rm/cyber/2004/binladen061704/segment1.ram)

110 "The Vice President Appears on NBC's Meet the Press". White House news release (Press release). The White House. 2001-12-09. (https://georgewbush-whitehouse.archives.gov/vicepresident/news-speeches/speeches/print/vp20011209.html)

111 Transcript for Sept. 14 - Meet the Press", MSNBC. (http://msnbc.msn.com/id/3080244/default.htm)

112 Landay, Jonathan S.; Warren P. Strobel; John Walcott (March 3, 2004). "Doubts Cast on Efforts to Link Saddam, al-Qaeda". Knight-Ridder. (https://

web.archive.org/web/20061208023017/http://www.commondreams.org/head-lines04/0303-01.htm)

113 Smith, Jeffrey (2007-04-06). "Hussein's Prewar Ties To Al-Qaeda Discounted". Washington Post. (https://www.washingtonpost.com/wp-dyn/content/article/2007/04/05/AR2007040502263.html)

114 Weisman, Jonathan (2006-09-10). "Saddam had no links to al-Qaeda". The Age. (http://www.theage.com.au/news/world/saddam-had-no-links-to-alqaeda/2006/09/09/1157222383981.html)

115 Grieve, Tim. "Welcome back, Tony", Salon.com, 04-30-2007. (http://www.salon.com/2007/04/30/snow_34/)

116 Ray McGovern, Proof Bush Fixed the Facts, TomPaine.com, May 4 2005

117 Joseph Curl (January 20, 2005). "Rise of 'dynasty' quick, far-reaching". The Washington Times. (https://web.archive.org/web/20060319124218/http://washtimes.com/national/20050119-123016-5212r.htm)

118 Toby Rogers, "Prescott Bush, $1,500,000 and Auschwitz: How the Bush Family Wealth Is Linked to the Jewish Holocaust", p.43

119 The Guradian, "How Bush's grandfather helped Hilter's rise to power", September 25, 2004 (https://www.theguardian.com/world/2004/sep/25/usa.secondworldwar)

120 Kitty Kelly, The Family, The Real Story of the Bush Dynasty, p 548

121 U.S. Senate, Committee on Foreign Relations; "The October Surprise: Allegations and the Circumstances Surrounding the Release of the American Hostages Held in Iran", U.S. Government Printing Office; Washington, DC., 1992

122 Uri Dowbenko, Bushwhacked, Conspiracy Digest, 2003, p 273

123 Gary Sick. 1991. October Surprise: America's Hostages in Iran and the Election of Ronald Reagan. New York: Random House.

124 Jeb! And the Bush Crime Family, Roger Stone, p 224

125 Affidavit of Eugene Hasenfus, #03575 in the Iran-Contra Collection, October 12, 1986 pp 2-3

126 Deposition of Michael Tolliver, Iran-Contra Report, May 1987, Vol 9

127 Jeb! And the Bush Crime Family, Roger Stone, p 236

128 North notebook entry, January 9, 1986

129 Terry Reed and John Cummings, Compromised: Clinton, Bush, and the CIA p 212

130 Al Martin, The Conspirators: Secrets of an Iran-Contra Insider, pp 195-198

131 Retired Green Beret Bo Gritz, Open Letter to George Bush, (http://serendipity.li/cia/gritz1.htm)

132 Nathaniel Blumberg, The Afternoon of March 30

133 "Bush's Son Was to Dine With Suspect's Brother." Houston Post, March 21, 1981

134 CBS 3 Philly, "Author Roger Stone's Latest Conspiracy Theory: George H.W. Bush Behind Reagan Assassination Attempt", January 28, 2016 (https://philadelphia.cbslocal.com/2016/01/28/author-roger-stones-latest-conspiracy-theory-george-h-w-bush-behind-reagan-assassination-attempt/)

135 Kitty Kelly, The Family, The Real Story of the Bush Dynasty p 787

136 Jeb! And the Bush Crime Family: The inside story of an American dynasty, Roger Stone, 2016 pg 252

137 John Nichols, Dick: The Main Who Is President, p 97-100

138 Peter Truell, Large Gurwin, False Profits: The Inside Story of BCCI, 1992

139 "A Mysterious Mover of Money and Planes." Time, June 4, 2001

140 Gregory Plast, "Bush Family Finances", November 26, 2000

141 Richard Clark, Against All Enemies: Inside America's War on Terror, p. 264

142 The 9/11 Commission Report p 39

143 Mitch Stacy, Florid School Where Bush Learned of the Attacks Reflects on Its Role in History, Associated Press, August 19, 2002.

144 The 9/11 Commission Report p 38

145 The 9/11 Commission Report p 38

146 The 9/11 Commission Report p 39

147 Susan Taylor Martin, Of Fact, Fiction: Bush 9/11, St. Petersburg Times, July 4, 2004.

148 Thomas H. Kean and Lee H. Hamilton, Without Precedent: The Inside Story of the 9/11 Commission, p 54

149 Andrew Card, That if You Had to Tell The President, San Francisco Chronicle, September 11, 2002.

150 Bill Sammon, Fighting Back: The War on Terrorism: From Inside the Bush White House, pg 89-90

151 Vincent Warren, The 9/11 Decade and Decline of US Democracy, Center for Constitutional Rights, September 9, 2011.

152 Peter Van Buren, How the US Wrecked the Middle East

153 John Nichols, Dick: The Man Who Is President

154 Lou Debose and Jack Bernstein, Vice: Dick Cheney and the Hijacking of the American Presidency, p 100-101

155 Steve Coll, Ghost Wars: The Secret History of the CIA, Afghanistan, and bin Laden, from the Soviet Invasion to September 10, 2001, p 330.

156 Ahmed Rashid, Taliban: Militan Islam, Oil, and Fundamentalism in Central Asia., p 75-79, 163, 175.

157 David Ray Griffin, Bush and Cheney: How They Ruined America and the World, p 33

158 Jean-Brisard, Forbidden Truth: US-Taliban Secret Oil Diplomacy and the Failed Hunt for Bin Laden

159 George Arney, US 'Planned Attack on Taleban' (British spelling), BBC News, September 18, 2001.

160 David Ray Griffin, Bush and Cheney: How They Ruined America and the World, p 33

161 Day One Transcripts: 9/11 Commission Hearing, Washington Post, March 23, 2004.

162 London Times, July 17, 2002

163 Thomas D. Dupier, I've Always Been a Yankees Fan (Los Angeles: World Ahead Publishing, 2006) p 11

164 Thomas D. Dupier, I've Always Been a Yankees Fan (Los Angeles: World Ahead Publishing, 2006) p 145

165 Ambrose Evans-Pritchard, The Secret Life of Bill Clinton. Regnery Publishing, 1997, p 282

166 Barbara Olson, Hell to Pay, Regnery Publishing, 1999, p. 188

167 Martin Gross, The Great Whitewater Fiasco, Ballantine Books, 19994, p. 7

168 Barbara Olson, Hell to Pay, Regnery Publishing, 1999, p. 143

169 Martin Gross, The Great Whitewater Fiasco, Ballantine Books, 19994, p. 104

170 Barbara Olson, Hell to Pay, Regnery Publishing, 1999, p. 142

171 Ambrose Evans-Pritchard, The Secret Life of Bill Clinton. Regnery Publishing, 1997, p 281

172 Ambrose Evans-Pritchard, The Secret Life of Bill Clinton. Regnery Publishing, 1997, p 282

173 Ambrose Evans-Pritchard, The Secret Life of Bill Clinton. Regnery Publishing, 1997, p xii

174 James B. Stewart, Blood Sport (New York: Touchstone Books, 1996), p 121

175 Hillary (and Bill): The Sex Volume, Part One of the Clinton Trilogy, by Victor Thorn, pg 16-17, 2008

176 Roger Morris, Partners in Power, 1996, p. 393

177 Al Martin, The Conspirators: Secrets of an Iran-Contra Insider, pp 195-198

178 Ambrose Evans-Pritchard, The Secret Life of Bill Clinton. Regnery Publishing, 1997, p 334-335

179 Victor Thorn, Hillary (and Bill): The Drugs Volume, Part Two of the Clinton Trilogy, p 156

180 Victor Thorn, Hillary (and Bill): The Drugs Volume, Part Two of the Clinton Trilogy, p 156

181 David Bresnahan, Damage Control, p. 76

182 R. Emmett Tyrrell, Boy Clinton, p. 12

183 Morris, Partners in Power, p 412

184 Denton, Morris, The Crimes of Mena, p 7

185 Denton, Morris, The Crimes of Mena, p 7

186 Evans-Pritchard, The Secret Life of Bill Clinton, p 30

187 Kenn Thomas, Parapolitics, p 182

188 Mara Leveritt, The Boys on the Tracks, p 310

189 Terry Reed & John Cummings, Compromised, p 232

190 Craig Roberts, The Medusa File, p 353-354

191 Evans-Pritchard, The Secret Life of Bill Clinton, p 311

192 David Bresnahan, Damage Control, p.48

193 Mara Leveritt, The Boys on the Tracks, p 209

194 John Dee, Snow Job, p. 4

195 Jeff Gerth, "Clintons Joined S.& L. Operator In an Ozark Real-Estate Venture", New York Times, March 8, 1992. (https://select.nytimes.com/gst/abstract.html?res=F10614FC345C0C7B8CDDAA0894DA494D81)

196 Investor's Business Daily (https://www.investors.com/politics/editorials/clinton-destroyed-whitewater-records-long-before-benghazi/)

197 "Caught in the Whitewater Quagmire", Washington Post, August 28, 1995; Page A01] (https://www.washingtonpost.com/wp-srv/politics/special/whitewater/stories/wwtr950828.htm)

198 Pardons by President Clinton, Wikipedia (https://en.wikipedia.org/wiki/List_of_people_pardoned_by_Bill_Clinton#Pardons)

199 James B. Stewart, Blood Sport (New York: Touchstone Books, 1996), p 35

200 Devon Jackson, Conspiranoia, p 279

201 John Austin, Rkansides, p 123

202 Jim Norman, Fostergate, p 1

203 Michael Isikoff, Uncovering Clinton, p 132

204 Michael Kellett, The Murder of Vince Foster, p 30

205 George Carpozi, Clinton Confidential, p 465

206 Christopher Ruddy, Vincent Foster: The Ruddy Investigation, p 135

207 Christopher Ruddy, Vincent Foster: The Ruddy Investigation, p 136

208 Christopher Ruddy, Vincent Foster: The Ruddy Investigation, p 169

209 Kellet, The Murder of Vince Foster, p 147

210 John Austin, Rkansides, p 124

211 Kellet, The Murder of Vince Foster, p 147

212 Christopher Ruddy, Vincent Foster: The Ruddy Investigation, p x

213 Victor Thorn, Hillary (and Bill) The Murder Volume: Part Three of the Clinton Thrilogy, p 95

214 Richard Odom, Circle of Death p 38

215 Patrick Matrisciana, The Clinton Chronicles Book, p 128

216 Daniel Halper, Clinton, Inc.: The Audacious Rebuilding of a Political Machine, p 55

217 Roger Stone, The Clinton's War on Women, p 40

218 Romano, Lois; Baker, Peter (February 20, 1999). "Another Clinton Accuser Goes Public". Washington Post. (https://www.washingtonpost.com/wp-srv/politics/special/clinton/stories/janedoe022099.htm)

219 The Washington Times. "Leslie Millwee, former reporter, accuses Bill Clinton of sexual assault 'on three occasions' in 1980". (https://www.washingtontimes.com/news/2016/oct/19/leslie-millwee-former-reporter-accuses-bill-clinto/)

220 Graves, Florence; Sharkey, Jacqueline E. (April 29, 1999). "Starr and Willey: The Untold Story". The Nation. (https://www.thenation.com/article/starr-and-

willey-untold-story/)

221 Roger Stone, The Clinton's War on Women, p 59

222 Clinton v. Jones, No. 95-1853 U.S. (May 27, 1997). (http://laws.findlaw.com/us/000/95-1853.html)

223 The American Spectator, His Cheatin' Heart, David Brock

224 Interview with Larry Patterson, The Clinton Chronicles

225 Actress Who Claimed Sex with Bill Says IRS Is Hounding Her, New York Post, January 23, 1999

226 Bill and Hillary Clinton's Latest Scandal?, Men's News Daily, December 23, 2005

227 Hillary Clinton's hired thugs quieted Bill Clinton's mistresses, Washington Times, R. Emmett Tyrrell Jr., October 4, 2016 (https://www.washingtontimes.com/news/2016/oct/4/hillary-clintons-hired-thugs-quieted-bill-clintons/)

228 Barbara Olson, Hell to Pay, p. 79

229 Richard Poe, Hillary's Secret War, p 27

230 Richard Poe, Hillary's Secret War, p 26

231 Richard Poe, Hillary's Secret War, p 26

232 Gawker Flight Logs of President Clinton and Mr. Epstein. (https://gawker.com/flight-logs-put-clinton-dershowitz-on-pedophile-billio-1681039971)

233 Douglas Ernst, Saturday, May 14, 2016 The Washington Times (https://www.washingtontimes.com/news/2016/may/14/bill-clinton-ditched-secret-service-on-multiple-lo/)

234 Malia Zimmerman, Fox News May 13, 2016 (https://www.foxnews.com/us/2016/05/13/flight-logs-show-bill-clinton-flew-on-sex-offenders-jet-much-more-than-previously-known.html)

235 John T. Bennett, Report: Bill Clinton Flew on Disgraced Donor's Jet 26 Times, May 13, 2016

236 Weiss, Philip (December 10, 2007). "The Fantasist". New York. (https://web.archive.org/web/20161017175912/http://nymag.com/news/features/41826/)

237 "Billionaire in Palm Beach sex scandal; Investigators: Moneyman Jeffrey Epstein solicited teen masseuses". Smoking Gun. July 26, 2006. (https://web.archive.org/web/20150112112028/http://thesmokinggun.com/documents/sex/billionaire-palm-beach-sex-scandal)

238 Malia Zimmerman, Fox News May 13, 2016 (http://www.foxnews.com/us/2016/05/13/flight-logs-show-bill-clinton-flew-on-sex-offenders-jet-much-more-than-previously-known.html)

239 Lewis, Paul; Swaine, Jon (January 10, 2015). "Jeffrey Epstein: Inside the decade of scandal entangling Prince Andrew". Guardian. (http://www.theguardian.com/world/2015/jan/10/jeffrey-epstein-decade-scandal-prince-andrew)

240 Roger Stone, The Clinton's War on Women, p 122

241 Associated Press, Many donors to Clinton Foundation met with her at State (https://apnews.com/82df550e1ec646098b434f7d5771f625)

242 Van Natta, Don, Jr., Jo Becker, and Mike McIntire, "In His Charity and Her Politics, Many Clinton Donors Overlap," New York Times, December 19, 2007

243 Bolton, Alexander. "Cornyn: Clinton duped Congress during confirmation", The Hill (September 5, 2016). (http://thehill.com/homenews/senate/294376-cornyn-clinton-played-both-sides-of-foundation-debate-during-confirmation)

244 Blake, Aaron, "Hillary Clinton, the Clinton Foundation and the promises she made about it, explained", The Washington Post, September 2, 2016

245 Fred Lucas, 6 Key Elements in Understanding the Tangles Uranium One Scandal, The Daily Signal, November 16, 2017.

246 Becker and McIntire, Cash Flowed to Clinton Foundation

247 New York Times, Jo Becker and Mike McIntire, April 23, 2015 (https://www.nytimes.com/2015/04/24/us/cash-flowed-to-clinton-foundation-as-russians-pressed-for-control-of-uranium-company.html?_r=1)

248 Washington Post, 1,100 donors to a Canadian charity tied to Clinton Foundation remain secret, by Rosalind S. Helderman and Tom Hamburger, April 28, 2015 (https://www.washingtonpost.com/politics/1100-donors-to-a-canadian-charity-tied-to-clinton-foundation-remain-secret/2015/04/28/c3c0f374-edbc-11e4-8666-a1d756d0218e_story.html)

249 The Russia Hoax: The Illicit Scheme to Clear Hillary Clinton and Frame Donald Trump, Gregg Jarrett

250 Becker, Jo; McIntire, Mike (April 23, 2015). "Cash Flowed to Clinton Foundation Amid Russian Uranium Deal". The New York Times. (https://www.nytimes.com/2015/04/24/us/cash-flowed-to-clinton-foundation-as-russians-pressed-for-control-of-uranium-company.html?_r=1)

251 Associated Press, Many donors to Clinton Foundation met with her at State (https://apnews.com/82df550e1ec646098b434f7d5771f625)

252 Helderman, Rosalind S.; Hamburger, Tom; Rich, Steven (February 18, 2015). "Clintons' foundation has raised nearly $2 billion – and some key questions". The Washington Post (https://www.washingtonpost.com/politics/clintons-raised-nearly-2-billion-for-foundation-since-2001/2015/02/18/b8425d88-a7cd-11e4-a7c2-03d37af98440_story.html)

253 "Clinton's charity confirms Qatar's $1 million gift while she was at State Dept". Reuters. November 4, 2016. (https://www.reuters.com/article/us-usa-election-foundation-idU.S.KBN12Z2SL)

254 John Solomon, "Uranium One Informant Makes Clinton Allegations to Congress"

255 Jessica Kwong, "Russi Routed Millions to Influence Clinton in Uranium Deal, Informant Tells Congress," Newsweek, February 8, 2018; David Krayden, "FBI Informant: US Lobbyists Paid by Russia to Influence Clinton on Uranium One," Daily Caller, February 8, 2018; The Russia Hoax, The Illicit Scheme to Clear Hillary Clinton and Frame Donald Trump, Gregg Jarrett, 2018, p 77

256 Brooke Singman, "Uranium One Informant Says Moscow Paid Millions in Bid to Influence Clinton," Fox News, February 8, 2018; The Russia Hoax, The Illicit Scheme to Clear Hillary Clinton and Frame Donald Trump, Gregg Jarrett, 2018, p 77

257 Grimaldi, James V.; Ballhaus, Rebecca (February 17, 2015). "Foreign Government Gifts to Clinton Foundation on the Rise". The Wall Street Journal. (https://www.wsj.com/articles/foreign-government-gifts-to-clinton-foundation-on-the-rise-1424223031)

258 John Solomon and Alison Spann, FBI uncovered Russian bribery plot before Obama administration approved controversial nuclear deal with Moscow, The Hill, October 17, 2017.

259 Investor's Business Daily, January 1, 2017 (https://www.investors.com/politics/editorials/the-clinton-foundation-is-dead-but-the-case-against-hillary-isnt/)

260 DailyMail, by Khaleda Rahman, November 20, 2016 (http://www.dailymail.co.uk/news/article-3954720/Donations-Clinton-Foundation-plummet-

ed-amid-Hillary-s-failed-run-presidency.html)

261 The Observer, The Clinton Foundation Shuts Down Clinton Global Initiative, by Michael Saniato, January 15, 2017 (http://observer.com/2017/01/the-clinton-foundation-shuts-down-clinton-global-initiative/)

262 What They Said, Before and After the Attack in Libya, The New York Times, September 12, 2012

263 Ian Tuttle, Hillary Clinton's Benghazi Defense: It Depends on What the Mean of 'Lied' Is, National Review, November 5, 2015

264 Secretary of State Clinton's remarks at transfer of remains ceremony for Americans killed in Libya (transcript), The Washington Post, September 14, 2012.

265 Donovan Slack, Hillary Clinton condemns Benghazi attack, Politico, September 12, 2012.

266 Evolution of administration statements on Libya attack, Fox News, September 20, 2012

267 Susan Cornwell and Tabassum Zakaria, In Benghazi testimony, Petraeus says al-Qaeda role know early, Reuters, November 16, 2012.

268 Judicial Watch: Benghazi Documents Point to White House on Misleading Talking Points, Judicial Watch, April 29, 2017.

269 Stephen Hayes, Hillary Told Chelsea Truth about Benghazi, But Not American People, The Weekly Standard, October 22, 2015.

270 Jake Tapper, Documents Back up Claims of Requests for Greater Security in Benghazi, ABC News, October 19, 2012.

271 Sy Hersh, Benghazi Is a Huge Scandal . . . But Not for the Reason You Think, Washington Blog, April 15, 2014

272 Brad Hoff, Hillary Emails Reveal True Motive for Libya Intervention, Foreign Policy Journal, January 6, 2016

273 S.A. Miller, Obama admin blocked FBI probe of Clinton Foundation corruption: Report, Washington Times, August 11, 2014

274 Hillary Clinton: Private email set up for 'convenience'". BBC. (https://www.bbc.com/news/world-us-canada-31819843)

275 Report by FBI. "Clinton Email Investigation" - 9 and 10, September 2, 2016

276 "Revealed: Clinton's office was warned over private email use". (http://amer-ica.aljazeera.com/articles/2015/3/3/govt-cybersecurity-source-clintons-of-fice-warned-private-email-use.html)

277 "Hillary Clinton Is Criticized for Private Emails in State Dept. Review". The New York Times. May 26, 2016. (https://www.nytimes.com/2016/05/26/us/politics/state-department-hillary-clinton-emails.html)

278 "Clinton not technically sophisticated: FBI interview". CNBC. Retrieved September 7, 2016. (http://video.cnbc.com/gallery/?video=3000548237)

279 Report by FBI, "Clinton Email Investigation," p. 12 (" State Diplomatic Security Service [DS] instructed Clinton that because her office was in a SCIF [Sensitive Compartmented Information Facility], the user of mobile devices in her office was prohibited. Interviews of three former DS agents revealed Clin-ton stored her personal BlackBerry in a desk in DS 'Post 1',' which was located within the SCIF on Mahogany Row. State personnel were not authorized to bring their mobile devices into Post 1, as it was located within the SCIF.").

280 O'Harrow Jr., Robert. "How Clinton's email scandal took root", The Washing-ton Post", March 27, 2016. (https://www.washingtonpost.com/investigations/how-clintons-email-scandal-took-root/2016/03/27/ee301168-e162-11e5-846c-10191d1fc4ec_story.html)

281 Report by FBI, "Clinton Email Investigation," p.18, September 2, 106; Byron York, "From FBI Fragments, A Question: Did Team Clinton Destroy Evi-dence Under Subpoena," Washington Examiner, September 3, 2016; DeTroy Murdock, "Obstruction of Justice Haunts Hillary's Future," National Review, September 8, 2016.

282 Report by FBI, "Clinton Email Investigation," p 19, September 2, 106.

283 "Statement Regarding Subpoena Compliance and Server Determination by Former Secretary of State Hillary Clinton | Select Committee on Benghazi". Benghazi.house.gov. October 28, 2014. (http://benghazi.house.gov/news/press-releases/statement-regarding-subpoena-compliance-and-server-determina-tion-by-former)

284 "No Copies of Hillary Clinton Emails on Server Lawyer Says". The New York Times. (https://www.nytimes.com/2015/03/28/us/politics/no-copies-of-hillary-clinton-emails-on-server-lawyer-says.html)

285 "Select Committee Adds to Secretary Clinton's Public Email Record". Select Committee on Benghazi. (http://benghazi.house.gov/news/press-releases/select-committee-adds-to-secretary-clinton-s-public-email-record)

286 United States Code, 18 .U.S.C. 641, "Public Money, Property or Records"

287 Cohen, Kelly. "James Comey: Loretta Lynch told me not to call Clinton email probe an 'investigation'". Washington Examiner. (http://www.washington-examiner.com/james-comey-loretta-lynch-told-me-not-to-call-clinton-email-probe-an-investigation/article/2625335)

288 ABC News (2017-06-23). "Senate probes Loretta Lynch's alleged interference in Clinton investigation". ABC News. (http://abcnews.go.com/Politics/senate-probes-loretta-lynchs-alleged-interference-clinton-email/story?id=48237960)

289 The Russia Hoax: The Illicit Scheme to Clear Hillary Clinton and Frame Donald Trump, Gregg Jarrett, Interview with Doug Burns, former assistant U.S. attorney for the Eastern District of New York, March 23, 2018

290 The Russia Hoax: The Illicit Scheme to Clear Hillary Clinton and Frame Donald Trump, Gregg Jarrett, Interview with Steve Pomerantz, former assistant FBI Director, March 14, 2018

291 The Russia Hoax: The Illicit Scheme to Clear Hillary Clinton and Frame Donald Trump, Gregg Jarrett, Interview with Doug Burns, former assistant U.S. attorney for the Eastern District of New York, March 23, 2018

292 Matt Margolis, The Scandalous Presidency of Barack Obama, p 111-112

293 Judicial Watch: Huma Abedin Emails Reveal Transmission of Classified Information and Clinton Foundation Donors receiving Special Treatment from Clinton State Department, Judicial Watch, August 2, 2017.

294 New York Times, Cash Flowed to Clinton Foundation Amid Russian Uranium Deal, by Jo Becker and Mike McIntire, April 23, 2015 (https://www.nytimes.com/2015/04/24/us/cash-flowed-to-clinton-foundation-as-russians-pressed-for-control-of-uranium-company.html)

295 New York Times, Donations to the Clinton Foundation, and a Russian Uranium Takeover, by Wilson Andrews, April 22, 2015 (https://www.nytimes.com/interactive/2015/04/23/us/clinton-foundation-donations-uranium-investors.html)

296 Politico, Inside Hillary Clinton's Secret Takeover of the DNC, November 2, 2017 (https://www.politico.com/magazine/story/2017/11/02/clinton-brazile-hacks-2016-215774)

297 Federal Election Campaign Act (the Act): Contribution limits (https://www.fec.gov/help-candidates-and-committees/candidate-taking-receipts/contribution-limits/)

298 Politico, Inside Hillary Clinton's Secret Takeover of the DNC, November 2, 2017 (https://www.politico.com/magazine/story/2017/11/02/clinton-brazile-hacks-2016-215774)

299 Politico, Inside Hillary Clinton's Secret Takeover of the DNC, November 2, 2017 (https://www.politico.com/magazine/story/2017/11/02/clinton-brazile-hacks-2016-215774)

300 The BBC Online, Elizabeth Warren agrees Democratic race 'rigged' for Clinton, November 3, 2017 (https://www.bbc.com/news/world-us-canada-41850798)

301 Chip Reid, Obama Reneges on Health Care Transparency, CBS News, January 6, 2010

302 Matt Margolis, The Scandalous Presidency of Barack Obama, p 28

303 Angie Drobnic Holan, Lie of the Year: 'If you like your heath care plan, you can keep it', PolitiFact, December 12, 2013

304 Edmund Haislmaier and Doug Badger, How Obamacare Raised Premiums, The Heritage Foundation

305 Glenn Kessler, How much did HealthCare.gov cost?, The Washington Post, October 24, 2013 and updated on Dec 12, 2013.

306 Avik Roy, The Truth Comes Out: Obamacare's Website Enrolled A Grand Total Of Six People On Oct. 1, Forbes, November 1, 2013.

307 Joe Johns and Z. Byron Wolf, First on CNN: Obama administration warned about health care website, CNN, October 30, 2013.

308 Sharyl Attkisson, High security risk found after HealthCare.gov launch, CBS News, December 20, 2013

309 David Ray Griffin, Bush and Cheney: How They Ruined America and The World, p 92-93

310 Alan J. Kuperman, Obama's Libya Debacle, Foreign Affairs, March/April 2015.

311 Jim Lobe, US Neo-Cons Urge Libya Intervention, Al Jazeera, February 27, 2011

312 Robert Parry, The Necons Regroup on Libyan War, Consortium News, March 25, 2011

313 David Ray Griffin, Bush and Cheney: How They Ruined America and The World, p 93

314 Joshua Yasmeh, Libya Was Hillary's War. Here's The Proof, The Daily Wire, February 16, 2016

315 Hillary Clinton on Gaddafi, CBS News, October 20, 2011.

316 Alan J. Kuperman, Obama's Libya Debacle, Foreign Affairs, March/April 2015.

317 David Ray Griffin, Bush and Cheney: How They Ruined America and The World, p 94

318 Damien McElroy, CIA Running Arms Smuggling Team in Benghazi When Consulate Was Attacked, Telegraph August 2, 2013.

319 Alex Newman, Gadhafi's Gold-Money Plan Would Have Decasted Dollar, New American, November 11, 2011.

320 Diane Johnstone, Hillary Clinton, Queen of Chaos.

321 Leon Panetta, Worthy Fights: A Memoir of Leadership in War and Peace, p 354

322 David Ray Griffin, Bush and Cheney How They Ruined America and the World, p 97

323 Donald J. Trump, via Twitter, March 4, 2017, https://twitter.com/realDonaldTrump/status/837989835818287106

324 Pierre Thomas, Jack Date, Rhonda Schwartz, and Erin Dooley, FBI director James Comey asked Justice Department to refute Trump's wiretapping claims, sources say, ABC News, March 5, 2017

325 Matt Margolis, The Scandalous Presidency of Barak Obama, p 131

326 Matthew Boyle, Non-Denial 'Denial': Obama Response to Trump 'Wiretap' Claim Raises More Questions, Breitbart, March 4, 2017.

327 Eddie Scarry, New York Times downplays 'wire tapped data' in online story of Trump investigation, Washington Examiner, March 9, 2017

328 Maggie Haberman, Matthew Rosenberg, Matt Apuzzo, and Glenn Thrush, Michael Flynn Resigns as National Security Advisor, The New York Times, September 13, 2017

329 Matt Margolis, The Scandalous Presidency of Barak Obama, p 133

330 Evan Perez, Shimon Prokupecz, and Manu Raju, FBI used dossier allegations to bolster Trump-Russia investigation, CNN, April 18, 2017

331 Kenneth P. Vogel, The Trump Dossier: What We Know and Who Paid for It, The New York Times, October 25, 2017

332 Mark Hosenball and Johnathan Landay, US Congressional panel spar over 'Trump dossier' on Russia contacts, Reuters, October 10, 2017

333 James Comey's prepared testimony, CNN, June 8, 2017

334 Gage Cohen, FISA Surveillance Requests Are Almost Never Rejected, The Daily Caller, March 6, 2017.

335 James Rosen and Jake Gibson, Top DOJ official demoted amid probe of contacts with Trump dossier firm, Fox News, December 7, 2017.

336 Dinesh D'Souza, The Big Lie, p 14

337 Dinesh D'Souza, The Big Lie, p 15-16

338 Friedrich Hayek, The Road to Serfdom

339 Curtis Riess, Joseph Goebbels (London: Fonthill, 2015), 64-65

340 Edward S. Herman and Noam Chomsky, Manufacturing Consent: The Political Economy of the Mass Media

341 Richard Cohen, How to remove Trump from office, The Washington Post, January 9, 2017 (https://www.washingtonpost.com/opinions/how-to-remove-trump-from-office/2017/01/09/e119cc36-d698-11e6-9a36-1d296534b31e_story.html)

342 James Kirchick, If Trump wins, a coup isn't impossible here in the U.S., The Los Angeles Times, July 19, 2016 (https://www.latimes.com/opinion/op-ed/la-oe-kirchick-trump-coup-20160719-snap-story.html)

343 Jeffrey Kluger, Why So Many People Believe Conspiracy Theories, Time Magazine

Made in the USA
Middletown, DE
22 May 2020

95675853R00096